Blanket of Stars
Homeless Women in Santa Monica

ANGEL CITY PRESS

Blanket of Stars

Homeless Women in Santa Monica

Frances Noble

Photographs by
Ian Noble

ACP
ANGEL CITY PRESS

Introduction

They sit on the grass under trees in the parks. They sit in filthy cars in front of City Hall. They sit on benches: park benches, bus benches, benches on Third Street Promenade, benches on the Pier. They stand in doorways. They sleep in doorways. They rummage through trash cans. They panhandle. They visit with friends.

They move around. Walking, shuffling, staggering. Often looking down. Usually alone. Burdened by bags and backpacks; pushing shopping carts spilling over with their possessions.

They are distressed, calm, disoriented, rational, incoherent, articulate, filthy, clean, angry, forgiving, pretty, plain, resigned, hopeful, brave, afraid, unspoken to. They write poetry; they paint. They drink too much; they use drugs; they're sober. Their families don't know where they are; their families kicked them out; their families want them to come home. They come from far away; they are homegrown. They appreciate the kindness of strangers; they want to be left alone. They're ex-cons. They're churchgoers. They're old and they're young. They hate the cold, the rain, the wind; they stay out of the heat of the sun. They don't trust the police. They had a job once; they never worked. One grabs at people as she walks by. Another howls silently. Many talk to themselves when they think nobody is listening.

They're always poor.

They say they live outside because they don't qualify for assistance; they say they don't qualify for assistance because they aren't insane or a drunk or an addict; or they'll lose their freedom if they go inside; or they're afraid of the men at the shelters; or the bank stole all their money; or they're being followed by a man who assumes many shapes and identities; or the FBI and the CIA are after them; or they're helping the police find a serial killer; or nobody asked them if they wanted an apartment and there are no apartments available to them, anyway.

Many have a hard time knowing what they think, much less saying it, because their thoughts are muddled and their words don't come out right. They hear extra voices in their heads, see things the rest of us don't see, and believe things the rest of us don't believe.

Who are they? They are the homeless women of Santa Monica.

If you had told me that I'd see a woman old enough to be my mother sleeping outside on the ground, that I'd walk by her without shock, and, further, that I wouldn't stop to help her—I wouldn't have believed you. But that's what I did.

My family and I lived in Santa Monica, California, for more than thirty-five years. My children attended its schools, played on its local sports teams, went trick-or-treating on its streets, danced at its proms, and body-surfed in its bay.

We watched as local institutions eroded in the rising tide of increasing real estate values and gave way to trendier ventures. We saw Santa Monica change from an almost sleepy beach city to a hip destination.

And we witnessed some of the earliest appearances of homeless people on the city's streets.

It was more than twenty years ago. I especially remember three people—two men and one woman. The men were clearly mentally disabled, although one seemed more debilitated than the other and sat for hours gazing silently at his reflection in store windows. The woman, her face smeared with makeup, pushed a train of shopping carts down Wilshire Boulevard. The men are still homeless, their once-black hair tinged with gray. The woman only recently left the streets. In the past two decades, homeless people have become an increasingly fundamental and expected part of Santa Monica—like the ocean, the shopping, the traffic, the celebrities.

What can be done to help them?

In November of 2005, my son, Ian, and I started walking Santa Monica's 8.3 square miles, intending to interview as many homeless women as possible. We wanted to document their presence, to bear witness to their lives, to leave a tangible record of their individual words and faces so that they would not disappear from public memory—with the hope that the next time you see a homeless woman, you really see her.

We walked the east/west streets, the north/south streets, and the alleys in between; Palisades Park, Reed Park, Memorial Park, and the rest; parking lots of markets, drugstores, and small shopping centers; Santa Monica Place, Third Street Promenade, industrial culs-de-sac; the Pier (on top and under); along the oceanfront by the breaking waves, in the middle of the vast stretches of sand, and down the bike path. What we didn't walk, we drove. Many times. We roamed the city for more than a year.

We interviewed past and present city staff members, social service providers, mental health professionals, and Santa Monica citizens. We read twenty years of newspaper articles, official city reports, studies in professional journals, proposals by think tanks, and countless internet stories and news bulletins.

The numbers were staggering: approximately 88,000 homeless people "residing" in Los Angeles County; nationwide, over 720,000, more than at any time since the Great Depression. In 2006, the city of Santa Monica retained The Urban Institute, a think tank, to conduct a comprehensive program and system evaluation of its homeless delivery programs. The Urban Institute's report, entitled "Ending Homelessness in Santa Monica: Current Efforts and Recommended Next Steps," stated that an estimated 10,800 homeless people a year walked the city's streets, which translated into about 2,800 homeless people a day. Of these, about forty percent were women.

Homeless people in Santa Monica have become such a constant presence, such a part of the city's routine, that they are almost invisible. And homeless women tend to be the least visible of all.

They don't congregate in public places the way homeless men do; they are often alone and quiet, semi-hiding. Or their appearances and actions make us uncomfortable so we pretend we don't see them. It's easier to turn away. It's a relief. But once you allow yourself to see, and you don't look away or through them or beyond them, you will see them everywhere. Although it is estimated that one-third of homeless women are mentally ill, our interviews and observations indicate that the percentage could be much higher.

Still, only a very few don't get along well enough to ensure their survival. Most find food, they do not starve. However exposed or unpleasant, they find places to sleep. Even the chronically ill get themselves to bathrooms and keep themselves covered. But without outside assistance, for the vast majority, this is as good as it gets.

Of the women we interviewed, most can't take care of themselves by themselves. They won't have "normal" lives. They will never be able to hold down the kinds of jobs that provide even a modest living. They will require extensive financial and emotional and practical help. Help getting to the store, finding the right doctors, managing their money, learning to live inside, living around other people, negotiating their ways through a stressful and demanding world.

How did so many women end up homeless on the streets of an affluent city in the richest country in the history of the world? In many cases, the conditions that caused the women to slide into homelessness are constants: poverty, serious chronic physical or mental illnesses—separately or in combination—complicated by addictions and their social, economic, and political environments. Many have been deteriorating on the streets for years.

Serious chronic mental illness, as a cause of homelessness in women, is often misunderstood and difficult to remedy, and it complicates and clouds every aspect of a homeless woman's life. Either there are few places for mentally ill women to go for shelter and treatment or, when they go, they don't get the right kind of help. One place where mentally ill homeless women can go and be helped is the Daybreak Shelter in Santa Monica. Founded in 1987, Daybreak is the only local program designed for homeless women suffering from long-term debilitating mental illness. For a very few, very fortunate mentally ill homeless women, the Daybreak Shelter is the light at the end of a very dark tunnel. The Daybreak Shelter provides transitional shelter with on-site supportive services for six to nine months, its ultimate goal being to prepare women to live successfully in their own permanent housing.

Some of the homeless women we met, however, seem condemned to wander alone through the wilderness of their broken minds and bodies. They will be unable to negotiate the world around them. They will be victimized because they are vulnerable and confused. Like Carol in Palisades Park, who is bullied repeatedly by a man "for the fun of it" because "she's crazy," and has no defense but that provided by other people. What can she do when there's no one to help her?

Or Stephanie, on the sidewalk by Santa Monica Place, so disheveled and dirty that

I almost don't approach her because I think she may not want to speak to me or be able to understand me. How wrong I am! Stephanie, whose sweetness belies her appearance, speaks sadly of a beloved father who died when she was young. She says she's afraid she'll be sent back to a mental hospital. She says we saved her life by speaking to her because no one had spoken to her for two months. Stephanie looks very ill. She does not want us to call an ambulance for her. We never see her again.

There's Vanessa, a young, attractive woman with deep blue eyes and long thick brown hair, who calls herself Serendipity. Her tragic deterioration on the streets is visible to everyone but her. When we first meet Serendipity, she is gentle and quiet and seems to understand much of what we say. Later we see her standing still in one place for hours. In the last couple of years her terrors have multiplied. She shouts in the doorway of a Laundromat on Wilshire Boulevard, alarming everyone around her. She drags her ever-growing collection of bursting garbage bags up and down the city sidewalks. She is afraid to cross the street. But the most shocking transformation is her physical appearance. What used to be mere facial hair has grown into a beard. Someone seeing her for the first time may not be able to tell if she is a man or a woman. I don't see how her spirit can survive.

Many of the homeless women we encountered have long journeys ahead . . . and miles to go before they sleep. They are young and have more than their fair share of suffering still to come. Often, they're not just poor, but ill in body and mind; not just homeless, but without the education or skills to change their lives. In their twenties and thirties, they cannot look forward to a normal family life, to holidays, to a job, to friends, to the respect and admiration of their peers. Their road stretches out before them without pause, without a place to rest.

And for older women, like Anne at the lifeguard station—generous Anne who offered to share her small bag of candy with me—the end of the journey may be nearer, but it won't be easier. Anne's physical journey is hampered by feet that can't take her where she needs to go. Still, she manages to go back and forth between Santa Monica and Los Angeles's Skid Row. Each time we see her, Anne sits alone on a bench, wrapped in her worn black jacket with the hood covering her head.

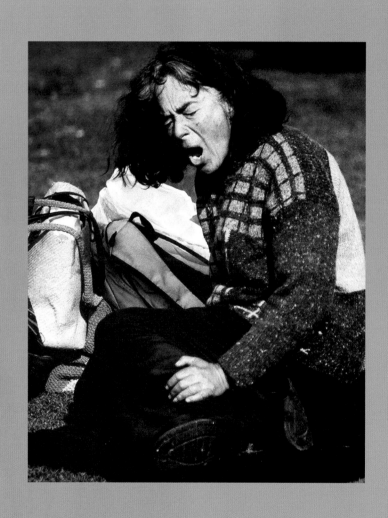

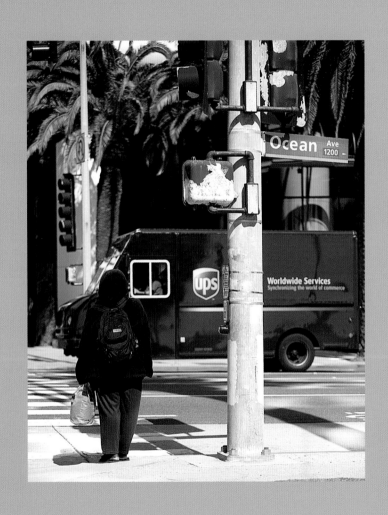

Other older women we meet are equally brave and resilient and strong. They don't ask for pity. They don't condemn us for letting them down. They don't remind us that we have cast them off in their old age. Betty is now eighty-two. Others are in their sixties and seventies. Mary (or Ruth, depending on what day you speak to her) tells us how she resents people thinking something's wrong with her just because she's older. There's Judy Marie, perfectly groomed and made up, who cheerfully displays the many prescription medications she needs to take every day. Cat and Nell are in wheelchairs. Is this how these women thought they'd live out the later years of their lives? When they were young, did they have dreams?

And yet more dreamers than you'd imagine live on the streets. What a gift—to believe in a dream under such circumstances. Sister Chi-Chi looks every bit a priestess of Isis. Charmaine writes poetry. And Star, calling herself Star because she's sure she can be one— like Selena or Jennifer Lopez or Mariah Carey. I will never forget seeing Star, in make-up and wig, glamorous and confident, singing into a wireless microphone while sitting on the barrel of the Civil War-era cannon in Palisades Park.

We also meet women so pure in heart and action we feel uplifted by their presences. Like saints of old, faced with unfathomable trials and challenges, they maintain an unshakeable faith in God and in life. Betty, seventy-nine when we speak with her, exhibits a radiance that can only come from inner peace. Her serenity would be notable in anyone, but in her, it is inspirational. She trusts in God and relies on the kindness of strangers, and it is easy to see why strangers reach out to help.

Francine and Kathy, two old friends whose lives embody the Golden Rule, whose mutual love and respect are apparent, sit under an umbrella in Palisades Park. Just visiting. We would all be fortunate to have friends like them, to be friends like them. Against great odds they have found peace and contentment.

Others touched our hearts. Young and delicate Janine with her beautiful manners who called me "Mrs. Noble" and told Ian to "take care of your mother;" Marian, who we would see periodically sitting on a grass hill south of the Pier and who would call out to us and ask how the book was coming.

But night always comes, and it is the hardest time to be a homeless woman.

Dangerous, unpredictable, frightening, miserably uncomfortable. Ian went out on the streets of Santa Monica night after night taking photographs. "It's a completely different city at night," he told me.

A woman reads a book by the light of a store window. Another walks alone along the streets looking for a place to settle in. Strangers sleep near each other, hoping for company, for safety. Two people who don't have beds turn themselves into beds, wrapping sheets around their bodies and faces to pass the night sitting erect on a bench on Santa Monica Boulevard.

And all long for morning.

Homelessness is one of the pressing topics of the day, but soon something else will compete for the attention of the body politic: the next natural disaster, terrorist attack, war, recession, depression, immigration scandal, school shooting. . .

And the world will continue to revolve while homeless women continue to sleep outside under a blanket of stars. The homeless women of Santa Monica are the homeless women everywhere.

Can you see them? Can you see her?

Every day a wilderness— no shade in sight.

—RITA DOVE
MUSEUM DUSTING (1983)

A jungle of sounds, images, and feelings with no way through; a daily existence of deprivation. Burdened with untreated physical and mental illness, many homeless women cannot help themselves to a better existence, to a more "normal" life. Without help, they are trapped in a wilderness of suffering.

Kittridge

November 30, 2005, early afternoon
Wilshire Boulevard at Sixth Street, in front of a 7-Eleven

What look like bags filled with junk and trash are piled on the stone bus bench. A middle-aged white woman stands near them. Her head is covered with a hat, but grayish hair peeks out. She is filthy and dressed in dirty clothes. On one hand, written in ink, is the word "Hate."

She speaks in disconnected words and phrases, sounding enraged. She speaks very, very fast in an unvarying tone. She appears unaware of my presence and of anything else outside herself. I ask her name and, although she acts like she doesn't hear me and continues her undifferentiated verbal stream for about a minute, she suddenly stops and says, "Kittridge."

Kittridge's voice changes when she says her own name. She says it in a normal volume and in a normal tone. And she doesn't sound angry when she says it. She also tells us in a normal voice that we do not have her permission to take her picture. She then reverts to her original demeanor and speech.

Kittridge says she is a doctor, a lawyer, and other things, much of which I can't understand. She doesn't respond to my questions, but speaks angrily in a stream of words that seem random, and moves about jerkily seeming alternately threatened and threatening. She won't look at me. Her speech and motion accelerate. "Leave the space," she says. We do.

Brandie

December 15, 2005
Third Street Promenade

Brandie's eyebrows are painted bright blue. She is a large, heavy, black woman apparently in her mid- to late forties. She is sitting on a bench in the first block of the Promenade. I sit down next to her and introduce myself. She loves my name because "Frances" is also the name for Frank Sinatra and she loves Frank Sinatra. Brandie says she is from Quebec and that she came to the United States after 9/11 on a Greyhound bus. Later she says she grew up in Mount Vernon.

Brandie says her name is hard to spell because it ends in "ie" — "*très difficile, pas facile.*" She used to get SSI (Supplemental Security Income), but no longer does since she was caught with a crack pipe. She says she was framed. She's had no money for a year and eats out of garbage cans. She's been told she has a bad attitude, and that she should "know her place." She says she used to have Section 8 housing. She "fought and bled" with the authorities not to have to take pills. She refuses to take lithium and believes she's incurable.

At this point, Brandie's expression changes from relative pleasantness to one filled with hate, fear, rage. Her face looks distorted and she lapses into profanity. She seems to see something behind me. She says it is a sign with writing on it. She sounds like she is trying to protect herself as she curses under her breath. When she remains agitated, I lean back to give her room.

I tell her it's time for me to leave and her face softens again and she seems to regain a sense of where she is. "Good-bye, Frances," she says sweetly. She tells me again how much she loves my name and that she wishes it were hers.

Carol

January 10, 2006, 11:00 a.m.
On a bench near the restroom near the Senior Recreation Center in Palisades Park

When I speak to Carol, she responds incoherently, uttering words I cannot follow. She jumps from one topic to another, even within sentences; the meanings of the nouns and verbs don't match. She can't seem to stop the flow once it starts.

This comes closest to what she told me:

Carol has had four husbands and is still married to the first; she has five children including a daughter in Portland, Maine. She lists numerous other cities and states whose significance I don't understand. If I ask a question, she goes off on another tangent. Yet she beams when I introduce her to Ian and tell her he is my son. And when I ask her name, she stops rambling and says, clearly, "Carol."

We ask if we can take her picture. She says we can. And for an instant, the expression on her face suggests she is aware of us. She looks sweet, almost coy. She half smiles in the direction of the camera and seems quite pleased by the attention. Afterwards, she reverts to her stream of unconnected thoughts and acts as though we aren't there.

A few minutes later, while talking, her facial expression drastically changes; she says, "There he is again" and "I don't like him." At first I assume she is hearing voices. But Ian and I look around and see a short, middle-aged Latino man, very clean in work clothes and baseball cap, standing beneath a nearby tree, leaning on it, and staring at her. We aren't sure what's going on, but he walks closer to her and starts touching her possessions. She gets very agitated, and we ask him to go away. He doesn't leave. His face is impassive. He continues to touch her things, and he shakes her cart. Carol is upset.

Ian tells him to leave. The man backs off slowly. Carol again indicates she is afraid of him. We talk to Carol for a few more minutes and leave. Ian turns around and sees that the man has returned to where Carol is sitting. Once again he begins to rattle and shake her cart and leans toward her. Ian goes back and tells him to get out of there. The man says, "Are you a police officer?" Ian says he isn't. The man says, "She's crazy," as if that explains why he can do what he is doing. Ian again tells him to leave her alone. The man walks away slowly, defiantly, watching us as he retreats.

Ian and I think the man is gone this time, so we start to leave. We turn back to look at Carol. The man appears about fifty feet or so down the sidewalk, comes out from behind a tree and again starts toward Carol. This time, Ian says we are going to call the police. I hold up my cell phone to demonstrate that I am calling 911. Carol is clearly afraid, and she

gets up and pushes her cart to another bench where a homeless black man is stretched out, apparently sleeping. He wakes up and asks what's the matter. Carol seems to know him. He thanks us "for caring" and tells us not to call the police . . . that he'll "take care of it." He says this a few times. It is clear that the Latino man does indeed think the black man will take care of it, and he finally leaves and doesn't return.

We see Carol many more times in the park. Each time her condition appears to be different. One time she sits on a bench close to the Pier with her hair pulled over her face. She talks to herself constantly as she combs her hair with a filthy comb. Her hair shows three-inch gray roots. She seems completely oblivious to her surroundings. She seems to have deteriorated greatly.

Another time we see her walking in the park, albeit very slowly. She looks clean, much more focused, and appears to be communicating with those around her.

Jay

On a cold December night, about 9:00 p.m.
Pavilions Market parking lot on Montana Avenue

A handsome woman who appears to be in her thirties comes up to me and asks for fifty cents as I start to walk toward the market door. She is slender and fair with nicely groomed long, light brown hair and moves gracefully. She says she is homeless. When I ask if she's gotten help from any social service agency, she says she can't ask for help because she's been "sodomized down under" and involved in government work "down under" and she gestures downward with her hand. She refers to conspiracies of various types of people out to get her—lesbians, gays, and blacks—and to a policeman who took her to the hospital at UCLA and raped her there.

Jay explains that she's from a well-to-do family in Tempe, Arizona, and that she lived with her sister in Maryland at Fort Mead when she started college. Then she diverts her gaze from me and her words drift off as though there's something she doesn't want to think about or say. She says her family hasn't seen her in several years, although she admits they would like to see her.

Unsolicited, Jay adds that she was molested as a child, but insists that has nothing to do with her current condition: her problem was not caused by being molested, but by seeing others molested. She thanks me again for the money and starts backing away, ending the conversation, and disappears into the night.

Deborah

January 23, 2006
On the parkway of Reed Park on Lincoln Boulevard

Deborah lies on the grass in the parkway on Ninth Street near Wilshire Boulevard. The entrance to Miles Playhouse in Reed Park is a few feet away. She appears to be middle-aged, has short straight brown hair and fair skin. She says she needs some fruit juice. I offer her my apple. She says she doesn't eat green or red ones, only yellow ones. I tell her she's in luck, that I have a Yellow Delicious with me. She takes it, looks at it, but doesn't eat it.

She says the reason she can't get up and walk is that she was put under a curse from sleeping in a garage the night before. She says that before last night, she could walk. I ask if we should call the paramedics, and she says no. Then her facial expression changes, and she seems very angry and curses us and tells us to go away. We leave. The next day we see her staggering down Second Street near Colorado Boulevard. Once she gets on Colorado Boulevard, she heads toward Palisades Park.

Lidy
January 17, 2006
On a grassy area near Sears on Colorado Boulevard

When I approach Lidy, she is writing diligently on a piece of paper. Later she explains she is writing various attorneys who owe her money. The first thing I notice about her is that her pupils are hugely dilated.

Lidy has been on the street for a total of sixteen years: in Santa Monica, in New York, in Pennsylvania, in Chicago, in New Jersey. She retired from work in 1992; among her jobs was working in the stockroom at Thrifty's—"now Rite-Aid," she points out. She was a member of the Retail Clerks International Union.

Lidy says she has cases against numerous lawyers and other entities. To present her claims, she was going to appear on Judge Wapner's show, but didn't. Nevertheless, a woman from his show came out and granted her a pension in Garden Grove Court in 1991. She's had seven attorneys and all owe her money, including one in New York and one who is retired. She lists claims against other people and businesses for money that has been stolen from her in various ways. She adds that her teeth were "messed up" by a dentist in Beverly Hills.

Lidy claims to be seventy-five years old and to have a grandmother who is 106 and hasn't a single gray hair. Later she says she is not getting the child support she should be getting for her two children. She mentions a twenty-eight-year-old daughter who is also homeless and has four children. Lidy says she can't help her. "What can I do?" she asks. Her second child is a son who is thirty and lives in Texas. Without a break in speech, she again declares that businesses have stolen property from her, including her Supplemental Security Income card and "other information," and that she's going to city council meetings to claim her money.

During the time we are talking, two men come up to us. Lidy knows them. One asks her for cigarettes and she gives some to him. The men's demeanor suggests that they are under the influence of alcohol or drugs. They hang around, so I tell them we'll be finished in a minute. They walk down the sidewalk, and once they turn back and look at us.

Stephanie

January 17, 2006, 4:00 p.m.
On the steps outside Burger King, Santa Monica Place

Stephanie is gaunt and dirty. Her smell hangs around her, an invisible cloud discernible from thirty feet away. She walks disjointedly, like her knees and hip sockets need oiling, toward a filthy sleeping bag lined with the ratty remains of a fur coat, and settles in—her face, a combination of despair and torment. She doesn't seem to notice people walking by. I almost don't approach her.

At first she is confused by my presence. She seems afraid and intimidated. But when I explain why I want to talk with her and tell her that I am writing a book about homeless women, she is touched by my interest. She does her best to answer my questions.

Stephanie says she is an artist who makes masterpieces. "Masterpieces," she repeats several times as emphatically as she can, given her clearly debilitated condition. Mostly, though, her words are as disconnected and disjointed as her walk. She has great difficulty stringing her thoughts together into meaningful sentences. She jumps from topic to topic and is hard to follow.

Stephanie shakes when she talks. She looks very sick, although she says she doesn't want paramedics or an ambulance. She is from Canoga Park, is divorced, and has two children. Her father died when she was twelve, and if he'd been around, she says, she probably wouldn't have gotten pregnant and wouldn't have had to get married. She speaks of her father in a soft, wistful voice. Obviously, she loved him and still misses him.

Stephanie says she is afraid of doctors and the authorities. She has been in a mental hospital and doesn't want to go back.

She says no one here has offered to help her. She says no one has spoken to her in two months, and she starts to cry. She says "you saved my life" by speaking to her and asking how she is doing. When she speaks and makes eye contact, a real sweetness comes through, and a longing to connect with other people, but her sense of hopelessness is overwhelming. We give her some money and the names of places to go for help. We never see her again.

Serendipity
February 17, 2006
Reed Park

She stands at the corner of Lincoln and Wilshire Boulevards holding a large stainless steel bowl. She wears a dark knitted hat and dark clothes; the bottom halves of her sleeves are almost in shreds. She is fair-skinned, dirty and unkempt and has a great deal of facial hair. She is smiling. She appears to be in her thirties. She says her name is Serendipity.

The park ranger tells us that Serendipity was evicted from Section 8 housing because she is a pack rat, and the stuffed bags in and on and around a shopping cart testify to that.

Serendipity says she went to high school in Orange County. She has not had any jobs and has lived outside for a year. She stays in Reed Park. She wants to cross Wilshire Boulevard, but she is afraid to because there is so much traffic. She smiles the whole time we talk. She also does not appear to understand much of what I say. She has had assistance from the Didi Hirsch Mental Health Center.

Serendipity doesn't want her picture taken because she needs a bath. She says if we want a picture of her, we can go to the City Housing Authority because they have lots of pictures of her. Throughout our conversation, her manner is mild, sweet, accommodating.

We see her several more times. A couple of months later, she is waiting on Ocean Avenue across the street from the Daybreak Drop-In Center. There is a fixed smile on her face; she doesn't seem aware of what's going on around her. She looks at me when I say hello. She is unable to carry on a conversation.

Later a worker at Daybreak tells us that Serendipity's real name is Vanessa. A different worker tells us that Vanessa is schizophrenic. We see her walking around town over a period of several months.

In November 2006, she is in Palisades Park. I walk over to say hello. Her change in appearance is stunning. What was mere facial hair before is now a beard covering much of her chin. She parks her shopping cart on the concrete in front of the women's lavatory. She bends down and rests her forehead against the cart that is piled high with her possessions. She doesn't want to talk to us. At first glance, it is difficult to tell if she is a man or a woman.

A week later I see her standing in the doorway of a Laundromat on Wilshire Boulevard, shouting about the rights of the citizens of the United States of America. She is extremely upset and sounds very angry.

We see Vanessa several times over the next couple of years. Because of her clothes and her facial hair, she could be mistaken for a man now. She seems even less aware of her surroundings, even less able to communicate with other people. She looks completely lost.

Sandra
Winter afternoon, 2006
Third Street Promenade

Sandra came here four months ago after a thirty-day hospital stay. She left without medical consent because she couldn't find her social worker, and she says people were stealing. Sandra's speech is slurred and slow, and I must listen carefully to understand her.

Sandra has had no schooling; she does not read. She wants to find her friend named Frederick. She didn't like the shelter she was in because it was dirty, and there were no towels and no soap, no toothpaste, no nothing.

Kelly
May 5, 2006, 4:00 p.m.
Palisades Park

Kelly is forty-nine. She has a nineteen-year-old son who works at a Brentwood market and a thirteen-year-old son she is not allowed to see.

During our conversation, Kelly names famous entertainers, politicians, and other public figures, whom she claims either owe her millions of dollars or violated her rights or person in some way. She describes being held by a SWAT team of thirty men at her house in Mandeville Canyon. She says it must have been an FBI SWAT team because she checked at the West Los Angeles police station, and they told her they don't have a SWAT team that big. She says sheriffs videotaped her eviction from the Mandeville Canyon house and that she had to leave behind her two dogs and a bird, but that Tibetan lamas have been sending her twenty dollars a week . . . so she's been all right.

Kelly says she grew up and attended college in Philadelphia, and that she also attended the Wharton School and New York University. She refers to a management business and a greeting card company that she owned.

She reports being involuntarily committed to the mental health wing of King-Drew Mental Center, which she describes as a nightmare. There was only one light bulb, and she was chained to a bed in a bikini. After that she was committed involuntarily again, this time at UCLA after she was involved in a rear-end automobile accident. She blames others for conspiring to have her committed.

Kelly is critical of police treatment of homeless people and of the facilities offered to homeless people. But not Daybreak. She thinks Daybreak is lovely space.

She said she has been prescribed several different medications and that sometimes people tell her she's mentally ill, but she doesn't think she is. She asks me, "Do you think I'm mentally ill?"

And miles to go before I sleep.

—ROBERT FROST
"STOPPING BY THE WOODS ON A SNOWY EVENING"

From across the country, from the cities and towns of California, homeless women travel to Santa Monica, bringing hope in varying degrees. Some seek a place to settle down; others are just traveling through. A few stay. Many rest a while and move on, their journeys unfinished.

Kimberly
January 10, 2006, 5:00 p.m.
Palisades Park

On a greenway near the sidewalk under a tree, Kimberly "tinkers"—her word—with a miniature pair of scissors, trying to fix them. Her bicycle loaded with bags is nearby.

She is a heavy-set white woman with red marks on her face like healing chicken pox. She wears casual clothes and a hat with the visor pulled down. Her straight brown hair is pulled back in a ponytail. She says she is nearly forty, but her full face looks younger. Kimberly is from Oregon and has been homeless off and on for four years. Kimberly looks down as she talks, and her speech is peppered with self-deprecating comments.

During one four-day period, she lost her job, her money, and her cell phone. She was so devastated, she can't remember what happened for the two months following. She went to a shelter and took her savings with her and gave it to a man for safekeeping. Instead he stole it. She tried to get her money back and was accused of stalking. She says that if she had that money, she could get off the streets.

Kimberly suffered from depression before she lived on the streets, and it's been more intense since she's been homeless. She gets medications from the Venice Family Clinic. She says she would love to get her teeth fixed, but can't afford to. The Venice Family Clinic can offer some dental work, but not all. She has never married and has no children. Her parents are dead. Although she has one brother and two sisters, she says she's out of touch with them now, although she mentions once trying to help her brother who lives in Phoenix. When she first came to LA from Phoenix, she ended up on Skid Row. It was terrible, she says.

Kimberly sleeps outside on private property near the police station. She's the only one the owner lets sleep there. One night while she was sleeping, a man attacked her. He attacked her with his fist, foot, and belt. She had a belt buckle imprint on her face. During the attack, he stood back and taunted her, saying he was going to kill her. Three police cars drove by, but they wouldn't stop when she tried to flag them down. Finally, someone called 911, and the police came and got the guy. He's now in jail. The incident occurred two blocks from the police department. A sergeant told her he wished he had more patrols cars where she was, but he doesn't. She says the man who attacked her was a "wing nut"—a phrase that means crazy. Kimberly is angry when I don't know the term.

She describes her life as "a lot of messing up." She's not interested in shelters anymore. She keeps some of her stuff in a storage facility. Kimberly seems on the verge of angry explosions during our conversation. When I express concern, though, she softens and seems grateful for the sympathy. Ian walks up to us, coming up partly behind her so that she doesn't see him, and she jumps with fear. She doesn't want her picture taken.

Kimberly says she has a good case manager now who's trying to help her get off General Relief and on to SSI (Supplemental Security Income) because there'll be much more money. Now, she only gets a little more than two hundred dollars each month. On SSI, she'll get about eight hundred dollars each month and that will make a difference for her. She seems very relieved that the case manager is helping her get appointments with the county and filling out applications and other paper work.

"Life's not fair for a person like me."

Carol
February 8, 2006
On the boardwalk just south of the Pier

Carol is forty-six. She studied to be a dancer, but her potential career ended at age nineteen when a car hit her. After the accident she lived in an apartment on her settlement check and Supplemental Security Income, but she lost the apartment when she had to give up SSI because of her lawsuit settlement. It took three years for her to learn to walk again. She gave up her son for adoption after the car accident.

She became depressed and started drinking again. She went to parties in Beverly Hills. She says "somebody took me in." In 1984, she got SSI back and got an apartment in Hollywood, which she eventually lost, too. Then she found out about Santa Monica. It seemed "really far." She came to Santa Monica with a boyfriend who later died.

She says she's been treated badly here. Once, after dark, she got a ticket for sleeping where she shouldn't. She says the only way to avoid getting a ticket is to hide while you're sleeping. She doesn't like most social services because they want proof and doctors' reports and are slow to help.

She mentions being arrested for having an open container of alcohol. As we speak, the smell of alcohol is on her breath.

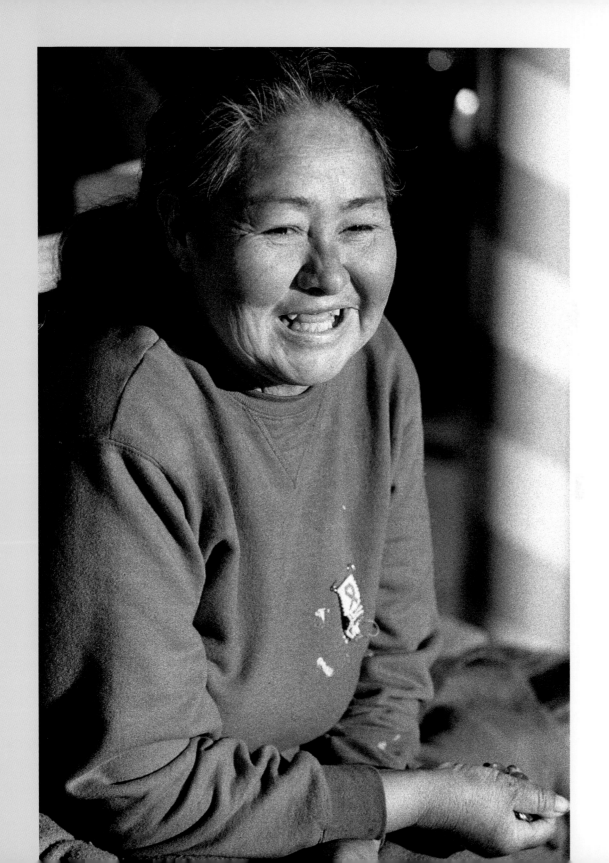

Phyllis
January 25, 2006
Palisades Park

Phyllis sits alone on the end of a park bench in the south end of Palisades Park, near the Pier. She is a fifty-year-old black woman. She last worked in 1999 as a clerk. Phyllis has been homeless in Santa Monica for two years; she was homeless in Long Beach for one year. She is from Oklahoma. She came to California fifteen years ago with her husband. Now she is divorced and has two children, but says they can't help her.

Phyllis wears a blue warm-up suit and red top. She is quite heavy. She says she comes from a dysfunctional family, and her parents are now dead. Three of her seven siblings are also dead. She says she has had two mental breakdowns and spent some time at Daybreak. She can't afford to pay rent. I mention a drop-in center where she can be inside during the day and have people to talk to. This makes her cry. She does not want her picture taken.

Anne

February 15, 2006
The wall by Lifeguard Tower 20, south of the Santa Monica Pier

Anne sits on the low concrete wall by Lifeguard Tower 20, her back to the ocean. She looks down at her feet, at the ground, at the bags next to her. A black woman who appears to be in her fifties or sixties, Anne says she was born in Italy although she grew up in Chicago in a home for girls. She didn't "look into" who her father was. She supports herself now by getting money from people. No government money. She got General Relief once, but now "there's no more coming."

Anne divides her time between the Union Rescue Mission in downtown Los Angeles and Santa Monica. She goes back and forth on the bus. She says she "owns" the special room at the Mission. She's been coming to Santa Monica for about five years.

In Santa Monica, she's stayed at two shelters. They were nice, she says, but too full. She finds it hard to get to restrooms and feeding programs because of her feet, which have plastic bags wrapped around them. She says that when she was sleeping, someone came and scratched her feet up. And they also tore up her shoes. She thinks they used their fingernails although she's never seen anyone.

Anne is the mother of a son and a daughter, now adults in their twenties. She hasn't seen them in a long time. She says her children went to private schools. Her daughter's name is Loretta.

While Anne talks, she takes an occasional bite of candy and she offers me some. She is sweet and soft-spoken and moves very little when she speaks. She has bad teeth, some of them missing. She wears a jacket with the hood pulled low around her face. Her body seems barely able to resist the pull of gravity.

Stephanie
April 21, 2006, Afternoon
Third Street Promenade

Stephanie came to California from Florida. She is twenty-nine years old and three months pregnant with her eighth child, although it is not discernible because of her weight and the clothes she wears. She says she lost one of her babies during her eighth month of pregnancy when her boyfriend pulled a gun and her grandmother shot him. During the altercation she says she fell on a shard of glass. She lived; the baby died.

Stephanie says her mother is a drug addict who kicked her out when she was thirteen; her father molested her when she was eight; she has been in and out of foster homes. Except for her grandmother, her family has disowned her. Her grandmother in Tallahassee takes care of her children, the oldest of whom is sixteen. As Stephanie speaks, she looks around without making eye contact with me. She says she is engaged to her unborn baby's father, and that he tries to take care of her. I ask what her plans are for taking care of the baby. She says she and her fiancé will get married and take care of the baby. He is currently in jail in downtown L.A.'s Twin Towers for a parole violation. He knows martial arts and hit her once, so she spit in his face. She was a member of a drop-in center, but she got kicked out permanently for fighting with another girl who tried to wake her up to go to dinner. Her mama, who has been in rehab multiple times, used to "slap her around." Stephanie says she fought back.

Stephanie is the oldest of six children. Her twin sister was killed in a car accident: all the kids were piled in one seat without seatbelts and her sister went through the windshield. Stephanie has nightmares about her twin sister, and says that their mama was laughing at the funeral. Stephanie mentions suffering serious injuries in a bike accident when she was fourteen; she stayed in intensive care for three weeks, and some man tried to pull the plug on her machine.

She graduated from high school in 1998. She loves to work and has worked in security. She also used to write poetry. Stephanie does not use crack, but she drinks a little. She takes medication for depression, and because she thinks about suicide. Stephanie gets Supplemental Security Income. She says she'd like to use birth control and in the past has discussed birth control with a case manager. She asked for shots, not pills, because she forgets to take the pills. She's been in mental institutions three or four times, once for two weeks. Several people have tried to persuade her to go home.

Celia
May 5, 2006, 3:00 p.m.
Palisades Park

Celia was born in Ohio. Her parents worked in the fields, driving a tractor and a truck. When she was four or five, her family moved to Texas. Later they moved to Oregon where they lived in a new, nice house.

Celia completed tenth grade. She started taking speed in junior high school and skipping class. Like her oldest sister, she got pregnant at eighteen and had a daughter, whom she named Angel. Her parents offered to take care of Angel, but Celia refused. Angel was legally removed from Celia's custody when she was six, and Celia hasn't seen her since 1996.

From Yakima, Washington, Celia traveled to Indio, California, and then to Santa Monica, where she has been living for the last six years. She said she got Section 8 housing and was the "happiest girl in the USA." But she "messed up." She let her boyfriend stay there, and he was on drugs, so she lost her apartment. He was in a drug diversion program and on probation and got sent back to jail.

Celia is bi-polar and takes various medications. If she doesn't take them, she gets angry, she has mood swings, and she hears voices. She was kicked out of one drop-in center for fighting with another woman.

Celia says the Santa Monica police have given her tickets for smoking and camping in the park. She complains that she can only smoke on the sidewalk now.

San Diego Woman

February 15, 2006, 2:15 p.m.
Palisades Park

A young black woman stands by the restroom. She took a train from San Diego to Los Angeles and a bus from Los Angeles to Santa Monica. She has been in Santa Monica before. Once she was homeless here for a few weeks. She looked up Santa Monica social services on the Internet and decided to come here again. Her last job was with a temporary employment agency.

She was born in Florida and is thirty-two, which might be young for a man, she tells me, but it is old for a woman. She says she feels sixty. She refers to a mental illness, which she knows is not her fault, but insists she is still responsible for her own life. At first she says she has no family, and later she says they tried to help her, but she owes them money. Now she is all on her own.

She has always had trouble making friends. No matter how hard she tries, it never works out. So she has given up trying; it apparently just isn't for her. I tell her about a local place to go for help and she asks for the address and for directions, saying she'll definitely go there. She won't take any money because she still has some left. She walks down the sidewalk in the direction of Wilshire Boulevard—her pace slow, her footsteps heavy. She never tells us her name.

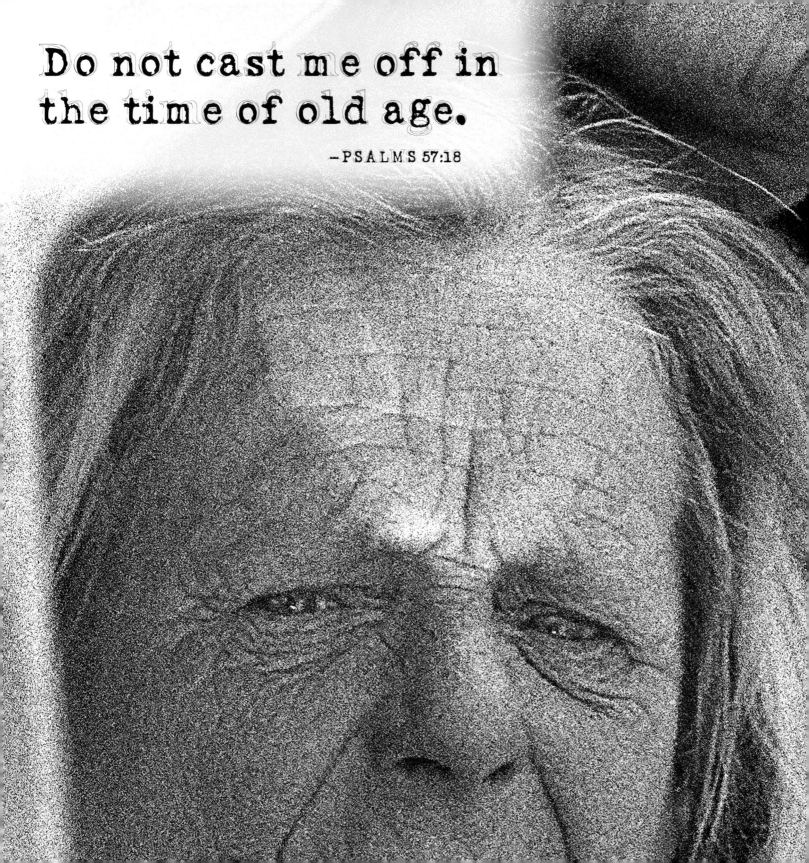

Do not cast me off in the time of old age.

–PSALMS 57:18

Women old enough to be your mother, your grandmother, your sister, your aunt. Sleeping on the ground on a bed of castoff blankets. When each woman wakes up, who will offer shelter? Or food? Or a companionable cup of tea?

Mary aka Ruth

November 11, 2005
Reed Park

Mary says the problem she faces is ageism. It used to be when she went to General Relief they'd ask how she was. Now they ask how sick are you? She attributes this to her age. Mary appears to be in her late sixties. She is wrapped head to foot in layers of clothes, and her head is covered by a hood. She could be heavy; she could be slender; we can't tell. She has blue eyes, wisps of once-blond hair peeking out, refined and regular features. She smells terrible. Her fingernails are long and filthy. When she smiles, we can see debris between her teeth. Still, it's clear she was lovely once.

She has been on the streets of Santa Monica for seven years. Before she was homeless, she worked in aerospace, then encountered the glass ceiling. Mary says she majored in chemistry and life sciences in college because her father told her to learn the hard sciences. She says she graduated from New York University in 1957. Mary came to California with her husband, from whom she is now divorced. When asked if she still sees her husband, she mentioned seeing him in a photograph in a newspaper.

I ask her how she could get off the streets. She says she could "apply for a grant or scholarship." She would like to get a job. She says to get shelter from a social service program, a person must be an inebriate or have what she calls "mental problems." Clearly she does not see herself in either category. She says too many tranquilizers make you go up and down—"It's the magnesium. You can go off like a spark on the Fourth of July."

When it rains, some churches, with volunteers of "all persuasions," help, she says, but modern churches don't believe in outreach per se. She wishes that in bad weather, church members would say, "We have an overhang over here for you to stay under." She says last year they were allowed to stay in the park until midnight if it was raining. Then she'd have to leave and find a "spot I could wish myself into." She says the general public should understand "everything is ease" for them. When the wind blows and it rains, her clothes stick to her skin.

She has a favorite eucalyptus tree in Palisades Park that she likes to sit under. She says "a comical thing" is that "occasionally I'll get my nose sniffed" by a dog. This clearly delights her. She's seen the same dog again and it seems to remember her. She tries to watch the sun set every day.

She says she lives a day-by-day "life in another's book." Life, according to Mary, is a combination of independence and curtailment. She describes herself as "fully independent" and then says she could use a little less independence.

Mary wanted to know what Ian thought about older people on the street. Did he think they were lazy? That if they worked harder, they wouldn't be there?

To sleep at night, Mary establishes her "ring of safety." She sits at a ninety-degree angle in a corner, so no one comes at her back. When asked if she's been attacked on the street, she rolls her eyes and turns her head away. In the night she asks herself, "How many hours are left?"

Ruth aka Mary

Week of January 15, 2006
Palisades Park

It takes me a few minutes to realize we have spoken to this woman before—on a cold morning when she was wearing layers of clothes. Today she's dressed for warmer weather, and her slenderness is apparent. Her long stringy gray hair, only partially covered by a pink ski cap, hangs below her shoulders. She wears eyeglasses so filthy she must not be able to see through them. One of the arms is attached to the lens frame with a string. She is still extremely dirty, but her teeth are much cleaner. She still loves to talk.

Today she tells us she studied cultural anthropology and attended Santa Monica College, San Diego State, USC, and UCLA. She had excellent jobs and spoke to school groups on scientific subjects. In 1996 her supervisor told her she needed help.

After her divorce, she became a non-citizen within a week when she couldn't afford groceries. Before that, she'd had an apartment; she was a "respectable citizen." She used to shop at Henshey's, a Santa Monica department store long closed.

Someone from the farmer's market gave her a free bag of oranges, but many of the oranges were stolen when she was sleeping. The eighteen-karat-gold watch her husband gave her was also stolen. Sometimes her bags are taken. The police found one of her bags in the trashcan.

The police ticket her often. Once she was running from a drunk, so she took refuge in the park. A policewoman approached her, shined a flashlight in her face, and said, "Stand where you are. Identify yourself." Ruth said "No" and got a ticket. She has had six or seven citations. The police hassle you, she says, although they've been nicer since the Rose Bowl, a change of behavior Ruth attributes to the presence of tourists. She says it will be worse for seniors in the future than for others.

She knows she doesn't smell right and she doesn't look right. Once she was standing near a store display window that fronts on an alley, looking at a lamp that looked like one her mother had had. A security guard stopped and asked her, "What are you doing here, peeing?" and made her leave. She was kicked out of the library after a woman with a baby complained of her presence.

She went to one shelter, an "alcoholic shelter," and there were only about ten women there. She said she was supposed to get two hot meals and a cot to sleep on, but she didn't. When she complained someone in charge said he'd kick her out or put her with the men. Ruth says women need housing just for women. Shelters have no room, and the waiting lists are long. Sometimes she goes to AA meetings because they let her stay inside where it's warm and eat the cookies.

Ruth says she is sad for guys in their forties who are homeless. They realize they're not going to have dreams.

Judy Marie
November 15, 2005
Palisades Park

Perfectly turned out Judy Marie sits on a blanket on the grass in Palisades Park. Judy is fifty-three years old. Her birthday is November 20. She is talkative and vivacious and eager to tell the details of her life.

On November 8, 1981, at three o'clock in the morning, Judy was kidnapped from her home in Wilmington, California, by her boyfriend, who was also the father of one of her children. The man was a longshoreman and meth addict. During the kidnapping, he crashed the car at Santa Fe Street in Anaheim. He was killed; she survived. The car caught on fire. A fireman kept a fire extinguisher spraying on her while the car burned and other firemen tried to get her out. She sustained terrible burns on the right side of her body; she has "no flesh on [her] hips." She lifted her clothes to show me the scar that had replaced her skin and muscle.

After the accident, Judy was in a coma for six months, and, since then, she has had many health problems. She takes medication for her heart, lungs, insomnia, ulcers, and blood pressure; she has additional prescriptions for pain, spasms, worry, and stress. She has an inhaler and gets pneumonia easily. She also has diabetes. She spilled the collection of bottles onto her blanket for us to see. She says she has had sixty-three surgeries. Normally she is in a wheelchair.

Judy says she is a manic depressive and, at one time, was a heroin and cocaine addict. Never alcohol, though. She has been clean and sober for five years, off heroin for nineteen years. She still smokes—her only remaining vice. Without explaining the apparent contradiction, she mentions that she is on probation for a drug violation. She was caught speeding down the Promenade in her wheel chair and also given a camping ticket, but her probation officer overlooked these violations. She has been treated at local mental health facilities. She has also been a patient at American Hospital, St. John's, Harbor General, Long Beach Memorial, and UCLA. She lost thirty-eight pounds in a recent hospital stay; she is very, very thin.

She says the state finally figured out it was more expensive to keep her on the street than to give her a place to live, and should be providing her housing in the near future. Judy keeps her things in storage in Santa Monica for a fee of $128 per month. Many homeless people do the same thing, she says. It's cheaper than paying for housing. Her cell phone costs her $99 a month; she calls it her "lifeline."

Judy was born in Hawaii. Her family settled in California in 1983, and she has been on Supplemental Security Income since then. When they first got here, they moved from hotel to hotel until they ran out of money. She dropped out of high school in ninth grade.

Judy has three children: ages thirteen, twenty-six, and twenty-nine. She lost custody of her thirteen-year-old daughter who is being raised by her sister. Judy says her sister is a "good Christian," so she's "fine with it." Her two older children live in Sacramento, but Judy can't live with them because she says she "can't breathe" up there. She left Sacramento in 2002 and came to Santa Monica, and she has been on the street ever since. She has been married four times: one husband is dead; one is in prison; one lives in Gardena, one in Pasadena.

Judy was kicked out of one of the shelters. She was "making a little noise" around 7:30 p.m. and was told to keep it down. Instead, she talked back. One of the men on staff swore at her and told her to get out of there.

Judy keeps going by looking at the positive. She attends Loveland Church in Santa Monica, and, when she needs medical care, she goes to the Venice Family Clinic, which she credits with keeping her alive for five years. She and two others sleep on private property with the permission of the owner; they can stay there if they keep it clean. Every morning she gets up at 4:00 and showers at the public showers at the Pier.

She continues to worry about how thin she is and especially about the flesh burned off in the flaming car crash of 1981: says she's "gotta go to Frederick's of Hollywood and get me a left side."

She knows she's on her own. "God's the only one that's at my back."

Olive
November 30, 2005
Second Street across from the Laemmle Theatre

Olive came to New York from Jamaica in 1969 to be with her mother and uncle. She came to California in 1989. She's been off the street for ten years; she was homeless from 1989 to 1995.

She's on crutches now because of injuries she suffered in an accident. She has no teeth, which makes it difficult to understand her when she speaks. She asks if my teeth are my own.

She says she was in jail once, but will say nothing further about it. She has four children whom she rarely sees. The government now pays for her housing and she lives in a board-and-care residence. In the past she went to a drop-in center for the mentally ill, but she doesn't like it now because it has gates. She says there are too many homeless people in California. One reason is that people get dumped from jail on to the street.

Olive smiles continually during our conversation. She is good-natured, humorous. She asks for cigarettes and we give her some. She likes getting her picture taken and strikes several different poses. As we leave, she says, "I enjoyed talking with you," and asks if we can bring her a Christmas present.

Marie
December 15, 2005
Third Street Promenade

Marie is engaging, good-humored, communicative. In the spirit of the season she wears a red Christmas cap while panhandling on the Promenade. She is one of the regulars.

During our conversation, she covers many different topics. She says in the past she had to have a guy arrested because, in front of a thousand people, he promised to murder her. He terrorized her, but she got him in court by preparing her own paperwork for the restraining order. Her cousin, who is a Texas Highway Patrol officer, served the legal papers on the guy when he was in a van.

Originally from New Mexico, Marie says she is related to Belle Star and that she saw Jesse James when he was dying. She is the sixth of seven daughters. She says Bonnie Parker was her mother's cousin, and that everyone in her family said she looked like Bonnie Parker.

Marie has been homeless for seven years. Three of those years have been spent in Santa Monica. She is on the city's housing list, but she doesn't know when she'll get a place. She says she was turned down by one program because she "wasn't nutty enough."

She says the ones who know how to use the system are crack addicts. She comments on another woman standing nearby who is also asking for money; this second woman is middle-aged and looks very vulnerable and probably mentally handicapped. Marie says this woman is taken advantage of by her landlady, that the landlady sends this other woman out to beg and when she gets home, takes all her money.

Marie cleans up in a bathroom at her storage unit using baby wipes. She recommends them for use by the military; they should use baby wipes if they can't get a shower.

Marie is sixty years old. She was born on August 7, 1945, and is a Leo. Her twin was stillborn. She thinks of this lost twin as her "missing link."

She says her cousin Jack comes by to see her every day about noon and lets her call her younger daughter. Her message to the world: "Don't ever give up."

Nell

January 9, 2006
Palisades Park

Nell is hunched over in her wheelchair, eating ice cream. When she is finished, she wheels over to a nearby trashcan to throw away the empty paper bowl and the plastic spoon. She moves herself forward with her feet—as though walking while sitting down.

After she finishes, she locates her wheelchair on the sidewalk and seems to be falling asleep or losing consciousness. She droops forward, leaning farther and farther. It looks as though she may fall out of the wheelchair and on to the cement. I go up to her and say "Madam" several times trying to wake her up before she gets hurt. All of a sudden she jerks up. "I'm reading," she snaps. Open flat on her lap is a small comic book that can't be seen from a few feet away.

I ask if I may talk to her. She nods. I ask her a few questions but can't understand much of what she says. It is difficult for her to speak; at first I think she may have had a stroke. I believe she said that she was in a car accident four years ago and, as a result of the accident, has been in the wheelchair for two years. She says she was on the street for two years after being kicked out of her hotel.

She says her name is Nell. In spite of her difficulty speaking, her sweetness comes through. When I ask her if we can photograph her, she agrees, and, looking pleased by the attention, smiles at the camera. She seems touched that someone wants to take her picture.

Libby

January 23, 2006, about 9:00 p.m.
Outside an entrance to the Main Library on Santa Monica Boulevard

Libby has great hair and a great haircut. Well turned out, focused, sharp. At first glance: a wealthy local matron, a literary agent, a community activist. She is in the entry to the library—but does not go inside. The library is closing. I notice she is wearing two pair of pants: the underneath pair is from a red warm-up suit, and there's a white stripe down the outside of the pant leg.

Libby is a self-described poet, smart and snappy in both her speech and demeanor. Sixty-five years of age and nine months; I.Q. 167. She says she became homeless this month, was kicked out by a landlord who "had a thing against her." Her cell phone was stolen and her son's phone number was in it. Although he lives five blocks away, she can't go there because his wife will call the police. She says her son has a temporary restraining order against her. She tells us that her bank stole her money and that she is not allowed to go into the library. She insists she's not paranoid.

She speaks with contempt of other people. She is angry. Her statements sound like challenges. She has tried four times to get Supplemental Security Income; she has tried to get into a shelter. She relates a negative interaction with a policewoman. Tomorrow she is going to the West Los Angeles public library where she has signed up for a two-hour computer session, and that's where she'll be if I want to talk with her further. She would clearly like to talk, to explain herself and her situation. She leaves, pulling a piece of luggage on wheels and smoking a cigarette.

Later in January 2006, 1:00 p.m.
Vons Market at Fourteenth Street and Wilshire Boulevard

I see Libby walking slowly down the sidewalk in the rain in front of the market. She wears a bright yellow knee-length rain poncho. She smokes a cigarette. She pulls her suitcase behind her.

October 2006, Afternoon
7-Eleven on Wilshire Boulevard

I say hello to Libby and ask if we can take her picture. She remembers me and is delighted. She poses in front of the flower stand.

Nancy
November 30, 2005, 4:30 p.m.
Third Street Promenade

A woman wearing multiple layers of clothes and a hood on her head sits on one of the metal benches on the Promenade. She is white and appears to be in her forties or fifties. She talks to herself when she thinks no one is listening. She seems pleased to talk to us. Her name is Nancy.

Nancy's been on the street since 2001 and would love to go "inside," but she's "not crazy enough or sick enough" to qualify for a program. Although she says if she's out here long enough, maybe she'll qualify. She grew up back east. She is divorced, and now her family is old or gone, although she has a brother. She says she has no one to help her. Then she says old friends and family members come by to visit with her.

She says she has a lawyer in Beverly Hills who's taking care of her legal matters, which have to do with family businesses. She used to run the businesses and was good at it, but it got to be too big a job. When these matters are taken care of, she'll have enough money to get off the street. Her lawyer contacts her by giving messages to a friend who comes to the Promenade and relays them to her.

A homeless man comes up to speak to her. She tells him to go away; she tells me he's crazy and she doesn't want to talk to him.

Nancy says she is "at a crossroads" and must make a decision about what she's going to do, where she's going to live. She must get back to work, get back into things. When I ask her what kind of work, she says she can do many things. As we continue to talk, she slips into responding to the voices she hears. But she insists she's not mentally ill. I ask her where she gets food, and she says some of the chefs on the Promenade are very good to her; so good to her, she "may as well be in the kitchen."

As we leave, she points to my bottle. "Don't forget your water," she says sweetly.

Name Withheld

April 21, 2006, Afternoon
In a doorway on the north side of Arizona Avenue near Seventh Street

She will not give her name nor tell me where she is from. She is heavy, in her sixties, and sits inside a doorway on Arizona Street near Seventh. She has no teeth. Her thick gray hair hangs just below her shoulders; her eyebrows look as though they've been plucked out and are just growing back. On her fingernails is chipped burgundy polish. She has the ruddy tan of a person who lives outside. She is surrounded by her things, including a shopping cart bursting with full plastic bags and bits of papers. She has been on the street in Santa Monica for a year.

She gets no government funds. She used to get Supplemental Security Income but doesn't now and won't say why. She intends to go back to the Supplemental Security Income office to see if she can again receive it. She used to have a walking stick, but it was stolen. Now, to walk, she must lean against something and move herself along. She is well spoken. Her face seems to register determination, hope, resignation, despair—all at once.

She doesn't like shelters. She just wants a room of her own.

Marian

February 2, 2006
On a grassy mound near the beach near Ocean Park Boulevard

On a blanket laid carefully over a tarp, Marian sits. But for the telltale bags of belongings on the ground near her, she could be anyone's elegant grandmother. Her black-and-white hair is neatly pulled back into a bun. Her peachy caramel skin showcases her beautiful white teeth that, she tells me later on, are dentures, since her own teeth "were shot." Her nails are manicured; she wears attractive jewelry and handsome clothes. She is articulate. Marian is sixty-seven years old.

Marian is a graduate of the University of California, Berkeley, and in a former life worked in Northern California as a family therapist and rehab counselor. Her father bought a home for her and, when she got married, put the deed in her and her husband's name. A great mistake, she says, because when they got divorced, she lost half its value. Due to cuts in the government budget, she became unemployed in the early 1980s and then lost her unemployment benefits. She went on welfare. She became homeless in the Bay Area even though she had friends and relatives there and has been homeless off and on ever since. While homeless in the Bay Area, she volunteered with the Gray Panthers.

Between periods of homelessness, Marian has had various types of housing. She stayed with convalescents in exchange for room and board; she lived with her mother and grandmother in Section 8 housing; she stayed with a daughter for a year and with her brother for a while in Northridge. She lived with her sister in an apartment in Los Angeles. After that she lived alone in a studio apartment for five years. In March of 2000, she signed up for a Section 8 housing voucher that came through in 2002. But the daughter who lives up north was having surgery, and Marian needed to care for her. She tried to transfer the voucher up north, but couldn't do it. She went to the housing authorities twice, and each time the woman she was supposed to see wasn't there. She was unable to get a thirty-day extension and lost the voucher.

Marian still keeps some of her things in a storage locker in Berkeley, although the monthly rent has been raised. She calls it "grand larceny" and shows me papers she received from the storage company.

Marian again mentions Cal Berkeley and says she was in the top ten percent of her class. When she was at Cal, the National Guard made Berkeley a war camp. Everywhere you

looked there were "goddam tear gas bombs." She says she was involved in the free speech movement. Did I know about the draft office being blown up, she asks? She says she became homeless because of politics, and her expression changes to one of intense anger. That intense expression lasts only a few seconds.

When she applied for General Relief and Supplemental Security Income, the doctors determined that she "couldn't function at full capacity." She believes it was because of all those years on the street. "Two or three state doctors" examined her and determined she was disabled. "They guessed my mental health was impaired."

Marian keeps two umbrellas for sleeping at night, especially if it's raining. Once she was sleeping on the sidewalk against a building on a cul-de-sac. There was no one else around. The police saw her and gave her a camping ticket and made her get up and move. It was around midnight. She went to court and the ticket was dismissed. Sometimes she sleeps with a group of five or six other homeless people in a covered lot. One night a man came along, also homeless, and said it was his spot. The others were afraid of him, so they all got up and left. It started to rain, so she went to a Laundromat. She has had two colds recently.

Marian speaks with poise and confidence and without a trace of self-pity or resentment. While she doesn't minimize the difficulties of living outside, she communicates an ability and a willingness to take care of herself and manage her life. As we speak, a man walking in the distance waves to her, and she waves back.

Cat
March 23, 2006
Third Street Promenade

Cat sits in a wheel chair on the Promenade. She is so soft-spoken I have to lean close to be able to hear her, and there are times during our conversation when I miss what she says.

Cat is an artist. She makes political cartoons, one of which she shows us. Her cartoon character is a cat—like her name. She likes cats; she used to rescue strays. She was born in an eastern state she prefers not to name. She came to California in the late sixties with her second husband. Her children are grown. They "have their own lives," and she has no contact with them.

Cat paints and writes poetry and has supported herself with her beadwork. Now she supports herself by panhandling. When I ask if she's held down regular work, she says, "Of course." She has been an apartment manager, a housekeeper, a home-health worker. She's in a wheelchair now because of steel rods in her legs. She was hit by a truck, which caused her injuries; she had the right of way.

Cat says she's not crazy and not on alcohol. She says she can take care of herself. She comes across as an intelligent, sensible woman. She has lived inside and outside and is now saving up for a place inside. She intends to do more artwork. She is future oriented, making plans for how she will manage financially and where she will be.

She says that what she has to say about social service agencies I wouldn't want to put in my book. She says some of the clients are okay, some are not good. Women are afraid of the men and of some of the women. She saw a dead man, folded over, on Skid Row in Los Angeles, and no one noticed. She says sometimes at the shelters males and females are put together in the same room to sleep. Guards are supposed to maintain order, but if the guard sleeps, things get stolen. She says she can get enough change to take care of herself.

Glory
Autumn, Daytime
Palisades Park

Glory was a nurse and speaks somewhat randomly about nursing and about other subjects during our short conversation. It is difficult to follow and understand some of what she says. She mentions her nursing duties, how doctors give orders and the nurses carry them out, how nurses know more than doctors, how nurses try to give patients what they need, how volunteer nurses get regular nurses in trouble. She says, "Off and on, nursing is punished."

Glory has been to Daybreak and St. John's Hospital. She tells us she knows better than to jaywalk. She talks about Venice and prejudice and surfers. She says the hardheaded won't go to shelters. She helps the old and young. She says people deserve respect, and there should be no assumptions about appearance.

She has one daughter back east. She describes a paranoid shouting man in downtown Los Angeles. She says it's like "kings and queens" here, meaning Santa Monica.

Lynn
Autumn Afternoon
On a bench by Norm's Restaurant on Lincoln Boulevard

Lynn used to work for RCA, doing wiring and soldering in Lackawanna, New York, but it was too cold there, so she moved to California.

Lynn has a son on disability, and they lived together until recently. She says she lost track of him and doesn't know where he is. She says he needs to lead his own life, and at the same time she says she wants to find him. "He went his way; I went mine." She also says she needs to find him so they can put their money together.

She seems confused about where she is. She says she's not sure where Palisades Park is or where OPCC is. She says she has to find someone named Roxie—they used to work together.

Several times during the next few days we see her sitting on the same bench. Her cat is in a container on the sidewalk near her. One day she is gone, and we do not see her again.

Linda

Winter, 2006
Third Street Promenade

Linda has been in Santa Monica for two years and says she has participated in a lot of good programs: OPCC, the Salvation Army, SWASHLOCK, Samoshel, feeding programs, public showers. She is from Indiana. She came here to work with a friend and worked as a waitress and in a grocery store, earning $221 a week.

Linda has six sisters and one brother and a half sister. She has no future plans. She can panhandle to get by, and she likes it in Santa Monica, particularly the beach. She says Santa Monica is much nicer than Los Angeles. Her family knows she is homeless and would take her in, but she wants to be independent. Linda is in her fifties and has three daughters, ages nineteen, twenty-nine, and thirty. She does not want to go back to Indiana; she chooses to stay in Santa Monica.

Behold, this dreamer cometh.

—EXODUS 37:19

She survives through the power of her imagination. Transcending the harsh details of her life by embracing her dreams instead of what she endures every day.

Charmaine

November 14, 2005, 9:00 a.m.
Reed Park

Charmaine is pretty and a little plump. She has olive skin and brown eyes, and her hair is covered by a hat. She is forty-five years old. She sits on a bench by the shuffleboard court, then walks slowly toward the trash can nearby. Another woman—tall, thin, older, jerking, and shaking her head so her shoulder-length stringy gray hair flies in the air, shouting incoherently—follows Charmaine.

A park ranger goes over to them. He is a very large man. When the thin woman will not stop talking, he shouts, "Quiet!" at her very loudly four or five times and stands menacingly over her. He threatens to put both women in jail, making no distinction between their behaviors. He tells them they are "making a mess of my park" and orders them to sit down. Charmaine does; the other woman does not. Charmaine holds very still and looks down.

Charmaine tries to explain to the ranger that the other woman has thrown her things in the trash. The ranger refuses to listen; he tells them both to gather their things and leave. Charmaine gathers her bags together and moves off the concrete. The thin woman has no bags with her. When she walks by me a few minutes later, she hisses profanities at me, tells me she recognizes me "from the sixties" and says that the concrete is made of "feces which will rise up."

Charmaine came to California from Idaho with her husband of seventeen years and their three children. After she was divorced two years ago, she lived in Orange County, and her ex-husband returned to Idaho with the children. She says her children found out what their father did to her, and now they are angry with him. She doesn't want her children to see her until she gets on her feet, and she has no contact with them or any of her family.

As we speak her eyes dart around and her head turns back and forth and she says she is afraid of the park ranger.

She doesn't like shelters. There are fights there and once she was threatened. She does not want to contact social agencies. She no longer goes to the library because she's only allowed to take one bag inside. She says she had two hundred dollars in an account in a local bank, and it's not there now. She believes somebody at the bank stole it. She says she could take care of herself better if she had that money. She touches her nose a couple of times with her finger. "Don't worry," she reassures us, "that's not a signal."

Charmaine is a Christian and believes in the Resurrection. She hopes to find a job, and she hopes to come back in her next life as a butterfly. Autumn is her favorite season. Charmaine writes poetry and has written a poem about lying on the grass in the park, enjoying the day, and appreciating its beauty. Like other people do.

Renee

January 17, 2006, 10:30 a.m.
Palisades Park

Renee sits barefoot on a bench near the Armed Services Memorial. She takes off her blouse to change and is naked from the waist up. She sits topless, unembarrassed. She removes the Scotch plaid turban that completely covers her head, which appears to have been shaved. She has pretty caramel skin and a butterfly tattoo.

At first she says she can't talk because she is getting ready to move her belongings from a tree to the bench about thirty feet away, and she can't talk and move her stuff at the same time. She has to think about what she is doing. Ian and I help her carry several large, heavy bags to the bench. She points to her things and says she's rich—otherwise, how could she have bought all this? Her bags are obviously worn—a suitcase, a backpack, other containers. She also has a bike, a bike lock, and a helmet.

Renee has been in California for two years. She says she is from Brazil and is an Indian—although she has no trace of an accent—and is a writer, a student of the arts, a poet, and an athlete. She likes to draw but can't always use her hands. She was a swimming teacher and a belly dancer. She loves the police and respects authority and is thrilled to realize that she'd put her things next to the military memorial. She is very handsome and looks younger than forty-eight.

Renee's mother worked, and Renee tried to help her by doing housework and taking care of her baby sister. She misses her baby sister so much. Her family didn't talk to her when she was at home. They closed the door to her room, and she was all by herself. She got tired of being in a room all by herself. Not that she blamed them—it was economic, she says. They had to talk on the phone and do things that didn't include her to take care of things financially. She insists this wasn't painful. Yet she tells us they weren't "intimate" with her, like she and I are being as we sit there in the park and talk. She likes being intimate. Renee left her family by choice.

"Light years ago" she experienced domestic violence, but she harbors no blame toward anyone. Life is "just the way it is." She saw a book that said "Hurt hurts people" which she really liked. She has never married.

Renee believes God sent her outside. She also says that since 9/11, there are more security cameras now and that they bother her. She understands the need for them, but they make her nervous and give her panic attacks. Renee loves the ocean. She does not want us to take her picture.

Star

December 15, 2005
Third Street Promenade

The first time I encounter Star she is sitting on a bench on the Promenade. She is jittery and seems nervous. She is hard to follow. She says she stayed at a battered women's home in Long Beach after enduring horrible beatings at the hand of her husband, a heroin addict, who also tried to kill her. They were married for seven years. She says she is from Kentucky and has two children. Later she says she came to California from Louisiana. As she speaks, she looks around as if she's watching for something; she expresses fear that someone will see her talking to me.

Star is trying to escape her sister's killer. Star's husband got her younger sister into drugs, and she was killed by a gang member a month ago. Her sister was thirty-nine at the time of her death; the killer is still at large. Star says she is afraid of gangs. "Gangs are no good." She says she is "being monitored in everything she says." She has a cell phone for safety.

She uses the name "Star" because she knows she could be a singing star, even though she hasn't tried it yet. She thinks she can be like Selena, J. Lo., and Mariah Carey.

February
Palisades Park

Star seems like a completely different person when we see her in February. Breezy, she rides her bike down the path like she owns the park. She is clearly in high spirits. I call out to her and she comes over and says hello. I remind her that we spoke a couple of months before, but that I didn't have the opportunity to take her picture. I don't know if she remembers speaking to me before, but she loves the idea of having her picture taken.

I walk next to her while she rides her bike, chatting the whole time. She says she has a new man, but is afraid God will punish her for being with him since they're not married. I suggest that God will be happy that she's happy. We arrive at a good place to take her picture. She laughs; she poses; she insists we have our picture taken together. She thoroughly enjoys the whole process. She is fun and funny, expansive and gay. We part with expressions of good cheer and well wishing.

A few weeks later, I see Star sitting on top of the huge cannon at the south end of Palisades Park. She holds a microphone and is singing into it.

Sister Chi-Chi
March 2006
Palisades Park

Sister Chi-Chi sits on a green metal bench in Palisades Park by the restrooms near the Senior Recreation Center. Next to her is a pair of pink suede moccasins with beads on the toes. She initiates the conversation, saying she won't be wearing the moccasins because they don't feel comfortable. She likes the sandals she's wearing much better, and she just had them repaired. She wonders what to do with the moccasins. She doesn't want them to go unused. She'd like to give them to someone who'll wear them.

Sister Chi-Chi says this "temple," as she refers to her body, was born in Nigeria. She had a past life in ancient Egypt as a priestess for the goddess Isis. She knows about this past life because she had a "life reading" and the reader told her so. She heard this reader on the radio in New York and got her phone number and called her. Sister Chi-Chi describes herself as a "priestess in the process of remembering."

In the recent past, Sister Chi-Chi worked on the boardwalk in Venice. She danced, sang, did readings, and sold merchandise. Living on Venice Beach forced her to proclaim to the world that she works for the Most High—a seven-day-a-week, twenty-four-hour-a-day gig. There's no paycheck. The universe pays her when the universe pays. She says she tries to be a channel of love and light. She sees everything as a test of her love and faith.

Sister Chi-Chi says she became homeless as a result of domestic violence. She left home taking her three youngest children with her. She got a list of potential shelters offering aid to domestic violence victims and called every one listed, and none had room for her and her three children. She says each one told her it didn't have a room with four beds. She also says the kind of cell phone she had couldn't get through to the domestic violence shelters from her neighborhood at King Boulevard and Normandie in Los Angeles. The domestic violence people really disappointed her; she says, "They don't work for God."

Sister Chi-Chi is the mother of five children. Her two oldest children, a son who is twenty-three and a daughter who is eighteen, live in New York. Her three youngest are in Los Angeles: two daughters, ages fifteen and thirteen, and a ten-year-old son. All three are in foster care. Sister Chi-Chi is allowed to visit them once a week although she hasn't seen them in months. She says the fifteen-year-old daughter refuses to see her.

Sister Chi-Chi has lived outside off and on since the 1990s. She came to California from New York in 1989. She says that her father was a journalist for the *Amsterdam News* and that her mother was a dietician. After her mother's uterus was taken out, though, she couldn't get another job. Sister Chi-Chi says that "a nutritionist that has truth should be able to have her uterus taken out" and that her mother remained unemployed as a "punishment."

Sister Chi-Chi suffers from depression. But she doesn't take pills for it. She says she's been punished by the local social service agencies because she won't take the pills. She treats her depression by being outside in the ocean air, not taking man-made medicine.

Sister Chi-Chi doesn't like the local shelters; they have too many rules. And some of her personal belongings were stolen, including a favorite book, for which she paid twenty-five dollars. It was a book about the goddess Isis with a beautiful picture on the cover.

Sister Chi-Chi is delighted to have her picture taken. She adjusts her clothes, removes her headpiece, smiles radiantly. She asks how she looks. She strikes different poses and positions. She faces the camera directly; she looks at it from an angle. She kisses the tree. She laughs and talks. She wants one of her pictures when they're developed.

Blessed are the pure of heart,
for they shall see God.

MATTHEW 5:3-10

Nobility of spirit, disarming innocence, radiant serenity.
How do these qualities survive and flourish in women
who bear the burdens of homelessness? Are they pure of
heart because they see God, or do they see God because
they are pure of heart?

Francine and Kathy

January 9, 2006, 9:00 a.m.
Palisades Park, near the Senior Recreation Center

When I first see them, I think they are simply middle-aged ladies having a visit in the park—two women sitting together on a bench overlooking the ocean. Kathy holds the open umbrella as though it is an elegant parasol, making sure her companion is as protected as she. The women smile and nod at each other, engrossed in their conversation. The affection they feel for each other is obvious from yards away. When I look closer I see that Francine has bags with her, unlike Kathy who is empty-handed except for the umbrella.

Kathy and Francine met in 1982 at Stella Maris, a Catholic residence for women on Figueroa Street in Los Angeles near USC. They lost touch and then, fairly recently, rediscovered each other in the park and have visited together since then. When we talk to them, they readily compliment each other and point out each other's fine qualities.

Francine

Francine is a black woman about fifty-five years old. She has a beautiful face and large, luminous eyes. She is missing some teeth; a few white whiskers grow on her chin. She is a vocational nurse by training, but, she says, she is a missionary, a spiritual leader, in her current vocation. Many times throughout our conversation, she quotes Scriptures; many times she describes the burdens she bears as tests from God and as evidence of God's love for her. She compares herself to Job. It is "God's desire for me to be out here, like Job. The devil tries to separate us from God. But we remain faithful. Matthew 6:24."

She left a church recently because the pastor tried to preach that Jesus wasn't homeless; she said the pastor tried to elevate the material world. She is a Seventh Day Adventist. She goes to church three times a week. She does missionary work on Thursday and goes to Bible study at a person's home. She's been in Santa Monica since 1999. She is sure that God will provide for her. She points out that Jesus Christ works through hardship.

God took away Job's ten children and his wealth and Job survived. She spreads the Word.

Francine believes that everything she hears or thinks comes from God. For example, God told her she had high blood pressure. He told her three times. At first she thought it was the devil talking. She was afraid it might be Satan, which she pronounces "say-tan." He first told her through "a young man's mouth." Then "God said go to the doctor because he knew 'his child' did not believe she had high blood pressure."

The doctor confirmed the diagnosis and wanted to put Francine on blood pressure medication. But Francine didn't want it. She wanted to eliminate the cause. She asked God to help her do what was necessary. The doctor gave Francine one and one-half months to lower her blood pressure without medication. Francine took care of the problem through diet and exercise.

Besides religion, Francine is knowledgeable about other things—the recent Rose Bowl game, for instance. She was interested in it because a doctor she once worked for treated college football players.

Francine has been married twice. She left her second husband because he was abusive. They were living in Lakewood, and one day Francine went into Newberry's and bought a suitcase and put her stuff in it and left. All she had was what she fit into the suitcase and the nursing uniform she was wearing for work. She has been living outside for many years.

Kathy

Her short bob, a wig in a color that is a combination of pale strawberry and gray, matches her ivory skin tone very well. Her skin is unusually lovely and she has expressive chestnut eyes. She is thin and delicate. Her hands are manicured—clear polish at the ends of long, slender fingers. She wears a scarf elegantly arranged around her neck, folded and tucked in. She is so attractive and engaging that I don't notice that she has no teeth until she mentions it.

As she speaks, she smiles continually in Francine's direction and Francine does the same to her. More than once, Kathy says how much she learns about God from Francine and what a pleasure it is to hear Francine's thoughts.

Kathy's speech is modulated. She is articulate and arranges her excellent vocabulary into perfectly grammatical sentences. Yet several times during our one-hour conversation she describes herself as "cognitively impaired" and talks of her "mental impairment."

Kathy was born in 1945. She worked as a legal secretary for a major nonprofit organization. She said she experienced great pressure on the job. When she became ill, she lost her job and had to "disconnect" from the world to survive. She had to leave life "in the shady lane" because those in the world made her feel bad. People she used to know weren't kind to her; they didn't help her or want to be around her. They didn't care what was happening to her. Illness and disability were not understood or accepted. She went her separate way a long time ago, and she's "doing fine." She learned to take care of herself. She learned to manage her illness and her "impaired cognition" on her own because she had no money and no doctors. What choice did she have? she asks. Here is the guideline she developed and follows: be aware of what makes you sick and what makes you well, and avoid things that make you sick.

She says she was diagnosed with depression but that the doctor was wrong. It wasn't depression she suffered from; it was narcolepsy. No one understood why she was dragging, why it was so hard for her to move and to take care of ordinary things.

After she lost her job, she couldn't pay rent and was evicted. An unlawful detainer action was brought against her to get her out of her apartment. She found herself homeless. After she was evicted, she tried to stay in emergency rooms at hospitals because she thought they were safe, but she found it terrifying to see so many injured and sick people. So she went to LAX and lived there from December 7, 1984 through February 15, 1985. Finally, when she was categorized as disabled, she began getting government aid.

She also says because she always worked so hard, she got less help. Her Supplemental Security Income payments were offset against other government support. She says it's "ironic" that after working so hard, she didn't get help when she needed it. She points out that she did nothing to deserve her situation, that it wasn't voluntary.

Kathy takes no medication. She is very sensitive to chemicals. She says the anti-depressant she was given years ago made her crazy, caused her to be bipolar, changed her ability to reason; she couldn't sleep at night. She says she "didn't have it together" then.

She has learned to be attuned to her body so that she knows what makes her feel well and what doesn't. When she walks she feels better, so she walks seven miles a day. In the morning at the ocean she walks four; she walks three in the afternoon. She walks to oxygenate. She decides what kind of oxygen she needs and walks. She has a good immune system so she doesn't get sick. Diet, exercise, journaling—these are the things she does for herself. She categorizes foods according to their goodness for her: certain foods are red and these are bad; green foods are good; blue are "hoho." She laughs at this last category, a word she made up.

She has had her own apartment in Santa Monica for a number of years. As it's turned out, Kathy says, she now has a sense of peace that she wouldn't have had but for the illness and hard times. She answers only to God and this makes her happy.

Betty

January 9, 2006
Palisades Park

Betty is seventy-nine years old. She is holding a torn Christmas card with a picture of the Madonna and child that she found in the trash. The first thing she says: do I believe in Jesus? Because if I don't, what could she possibly have to say to me?

Betty is Irish. Her mother, Rose, was an orphan and raised in a convent, but she became a Protestant because of the way she was treated by the nuns. Her mother instilled in her a belief in Jesus and came into her room at night and said her prayers with her. Betty has loving memories of her mother. Her mother married a show business man who was not accepted by her Irish family. Her father was a circus clown and also performed in vaudeville. She had a wealthy aunt and a grandmother who called everyone Betty, even a granddaughter named Grace.

Betty was born in East Los Angeles at General Hospital and lived in Maywood as a child. She attended Garfield High School. She is shy; growing up she had a girlfriend who was very outgoing, and so they were a good pair.

When Betty was a child, she met a man who was a "genuine hobo" and she gave him a potato. She knows you shouldn't talk to strangers, but sometimes a stranger is merely an "angel unaware." And if you don't talk to strangers, you might not meet the angel.

Betty was married for twenty-two years and then left her husband. She was afraid. She took her cat with her. Asked why she left her husband, she says she advises women to protect themselves. "Because things can happen in your own home, even by your own husband." All her family is dead now. "I'm what's left."

After Betty left, she kept going for the sake of her cat. She ran a newspaper stand for five years at Seventh and Broadway in Los Angeles. Then she did light housekeeping. When her cat died, she experienced deep grief and stayed for a month at the Sunshine Mission downtown when it was run by Mrs. Webber. She says it used to be a very nice place for women to go.

Betty begins her day by taking care of her grooming and then she finds something to eat. In the afternoon she takes a nap so she can sleep lightly at night. She goes through the trash because she likes to find good things. Once on the Promenade when she was going through the trash, she found two paper bags. She thought they had baked goods in them or something comparable. Instead, there were hundreds of dollars in cash in them. She was scared to death at the sight of all that money. "Any amount of money scares me." She took it to the police. They didn't have a "good attitude" toward her. They said they'd take care of it in the morning or later. From something on or inside the bags, Betty realized that the money belonged to a business on the Promenade. She insisted that the police return it that instant. They did. She refused "a cut" of the money when offered it by the owner of the business and seemed offended by the use of that phrase when she related the incident.

She says it's "like retirement here," meaning Santa Monica. "Like heaven," and that she has "never enjoyed a thing more." She's been here a number of years. "Happier than ever," she says.

Betty has no income. She has no desire for welfare or Supplemental Security Income. She depends on gifts from people she sees. Many offer her money. She trusts in Jesus to take care of her, and she believes He has. Once she put her life in the hands of the Lord, she had no worries, she says. She had a religious experience when she was thirty-nine. It was then she realized that Jesus would take care of her and she didn't need to be afraid. This faith governs her daily life. Even though she has been accosted on the streets and faced potential violence, she is not afraid. Her God is not far.

Most important, she says, is to be free. Though she doesn't know how young women make it on the street. She feels so sorry for them, for the dangers they face. She says if she had been on the street when she was young, she would have been suicidal. She's not sure she could have survived. Now that she's old, it's much easier. She says she's lived her life, "got my years," more than many have had, and she's grateful for that.

Christine

January 11, 2006, about 10:00 a.m.
Palisades Park

Christine has great vitality and charm and is open and talkative. She smiles readily and exudes good nature. She says she ran away from home to escape abuse when she was fifteen years old. Home was Baltimore, Maryland. She and a girlfriend hitchhiked across the country. This was in 1985. They came to Venice, California, looking for "cute guys." For a while she lived in Phoenix, where housing was more affordable. She says she's been on the street for years.

She says she was addicted to crack cocaine and alcohol but, through AA and self-help, has been sober for two years. She is bi-polar and suffers from anxiety for which she takes medications. She was given lithium when she was eighteen, but she became dehydrated and overdosed and had tremors. She is now a member of a drop-in center and leads an AA group there.

Christine's eyes fill with tears when she mentions her husband because he is now in jail. He was protecting her. A man insulted her, and her husband went after him with a machete. "If only he'd just hit him." Now he's awaiting trial on a charge of assault with a deadly weapon. The trial will take place at the Beverly Hills Courthouse. He has a public defender. Their two-year anniversary is February 19, 2006. She says her husband is "not the sanest man and has metal plate in his head." He spent twenty years in prison. She obviously loves him very much; she has the words "Mrs. B" tattooed on her arm.

Christine has studied cosmetology. She'd like to get her California license, but she says the test is harder here than elsewhere. She has earned her G.E.D. She sleeps at a local shelter.

Janine

February 8, 2006
On the beach south of the pier, afternoon

Janine is heartbreakingly young and heartbreakingly beautiful. She sits on the beach covering her head and face completely with a coat, which she removes after a few minutes.

I approach and introduce myself. She responds, "Nice to meet you, Mrs. Noble," in a manner and voice which suggests that she was brought up to be polite to her elders. Her manner is so delicate and sweet it is disarming. She looks up at me with chestnut brown eyes.

She seems very vulnerable and aware of her vulnerability. At first she says she lives in an apartment nearby with her grandfather, a statement she repeats several times during our conversation. She gestures with her head toward the buildings that line the boardwalk, suggesting that the apartment is in one of them. She sits there exposed, clearly without underwear; she looks dazed. She is very thin.

She says she is twenty-eight years old, though she looks like a teenager. Her birthday is October 7. She says she was raised in Malibu and went to Malibu High School. She says her parents are dead and that she has no brothers or sisters. She says she's studying psychology, archaeology, and fashion design. She refers to a fountain, an "old mermaid house," smiling as though this thought gives her pleasure. Her words are hard to follow and she has trouble following what I say. She says she needs a driver's license or a credit card.

Ian comes over, and I introduce him as my son. She says, "Now you take good care of your mother." We give her some money and walk down the beach; when we look back, she has packed up her stuff and walks unsteadily to a nearby food stand.

A few weeks later, we see Janine again. She looks healthier; she appears to have gained some weight. She is wearing clean clothes. She remembers us. She holds a child's toy, a pink plastic computer, on her lap and is trying to make it work. She says she thought it would be better than it is. Then she tells us, "No, it's fine; it's all right," as though she's not entitled to complain.

Mirela
May 5, 2006, 4:30 p.m.
Palisades Park

Mirela is from Romania. She is thirty-two. She is lovely and poised and seems very innocent. Originally, she came to New York to stay with a Romanian friend from her hometown, but he lived in a bad area, and his friends were strippers, so Mirela stayed there only a month.

Mirela worked at several jobs over the next couple of years—at a bakery in Queens, at a beauty supply shop in Brooklyn, at a bakery in Manhattan, at a diner. While working at the diner, one of the customers, a lawyer, asked her out, and she said no. The lawyer continued to come to the diner, and one time mentioned her rejection of him. Mirela interpreted what he said as a threat to "get even." After that, she believed she was being stalked.

She relates that different people followed her. They had many different faces and were of different nationalities. They looked at her, watched her. She was followed onto the subway; she was followed in Central Park. They followed her into stores. Everyone started to look at her. She saw the lawyer near her house, near the post office. She saw another guy wearing a black hood and wondered if he was the CIA.

Mirela made three complaints to the police department, but they told her they couldn't do anything. She went to the courthouse and asked a clerk what to do and was told she had to "wait for the guy to do something." Mirela was afraid and went back to live for a while with her Romanian friend. She said she was a good girl, pure and innocent, when she arrived in the United States.

She decided that a "biological mass weapon" was being used to watch her, to monitor her. It's the most intelligent mass weapon. It never stops. She mentions being in a hypnotic state, seeing others in the same state. She mentions being asleep, hearing loud music outside. She says that everyone is being watched and that when they are being watched, they are all connected. I ask her if we're being monitored as we speak to each other in the park. She says yes. She adds that somebody magnetizes the weapon so that all eyes turn toward her. She interjects that "schizophrenie" never existed. She tells us her conscience is clean and that a person with a clean conscience, like her, can defeat evil, which

she would like to do.

      Mirela's parents don't know she's homeless. Her brother knows, and he asks her, "Why don't you come home?"

      In November, we see a lone woman lying on the grass in front of City Hall. It is Mirela. She is still lovely—makeup on, hair combed and braided. I ask her if she is all right. She says she is. I ask her if she's gotten any help and she says no; she'd rather be alone.

Where you go, I will go.

—RUTH 1:16-18

At your side in sorrow and in joy, in the good times and in the bad, for better or for worse, for richer, for poorer, in sickness and in health ... Whatever the journey, it's sometimes easier when you're not alone.

Tina

December 2005
Third Street Promenade at Wilshire Boulevard

Tina's house in Missouri burned down, and she and her husband came to California to try to get back on their feet, leaving their three children behind with her sister. They had no money when they arrived. They worked at the Farmer's Market in Santa Monica for a time, but now they have no jobs.

Tina says it's very hard on the streets and that they run into threatening people at night. Her husband, who is nearby on the sidewalk, is much more assertive than she is when it comes to asking for money. She is happy to be photographed.

Months later, we see her again at the same location on the Promenade. This time, in a wheelchair. She broke her ankle. She again says we may take her picture.

Laura
February 2006, 2:45 in the afternoon
Third Street Promenade

Laura has been on the street for fifteen years. She stands alone at the north end of the Promenade, holding a paper cup and a small, hand-scribbled cardboard sign asking for help. She smells of alcohol. She has shoulder-length brown hair and blue eyes, a sprinkling of freckles, and is very attractive even with several missing teeth.

Before agreeing to talk, she says she has to ask her husband for permission. He sits on the edge of the nearby fountain. He gestures to her to go ahead; he seems impatient with her request. She makes a small curtsy in front of him and comes back to where I am standing.

Laura says she gets no public relief. She says she survives by panhandling. I start to ask her if she's been arrested for panhandling, only for some reason, I refer to panhandling as "begging"—the word surprises me as it comes out of my mouth. Laura snaps at me, "I see you've interviewed the homeless before." I say I have interviewed many. Angry, she walks away, down the sidewalk, east on Wilshire Boulevard.

A few weeks later I see her in the same place. This time one of her hands is wrapped in an elaborate gauze bandage and her lip is split and has sores on it. There appears to be a faded bruise on another part of her face. She talks animatedly with another homeless person.

Cynthia

February 10, 2006

Outside the post office on Wilshire Boulevard near Fourteenth Street

Cynthia stands on the sidewalk in front of the post office holding a piece of cardboard on which is written: *Hungry Help Thank you*. She gets in a fight with a blond man who appears disheveled and is probably also homeless. They start swearing at each other; her words come out in cackles and hisses. The man grabs at her sign. They go back and forth—hitting, cursing. It looks as though the argument will escalate. Someone inside the post office calls the police.

Two tall young officers arrive and separate the fighting pair, making them sit apart on the sidewalk. Cynthia tells one of the officers that she is five foot three and one-half inches tall and that she weighs 111 pounds.

After the police leave, Cynthia is delighted to talk to me. She says she's been on the street since 1984. The man she was fighting with is Wade; they have been together for the last eighteen months. They take care of each other, she says. She also says it's "chaos" outside—a word she uses repeatedly during our conversation. She smells strongly of alcohol.

Cynthia started out on the street with her former husband, but she left him because she got tired of being beaten. Her husband is dead now. She has a twenty-two-year-old daughter who was raised by her mother. Her daughter is now in college. Cynthia comes from Texas although she's been in Santa Monica a long time. She attended a Santa Monica continuation high school, up to the tenth grade, leaving because she had to work.

Cynthia sleeps in doorways on Wilshire near Tenth Street. She doesn't like shelters because they're too chaotic. Now she's running out of money and it's hard times. There are no more sack lunches out there.

Cynthia says she and Wade were fighting because they were stressed out and because he would not give her the quarter that she asked for. During our conversation, he held it out to her and she took it. She says people on the street will fight over a cup of coffee.

Wade looks a little younger than Cynthia. He has shoulder-length blond hair; he is dirty. He has dried blood in one nostril. He refers to their argument, saying he "did it on purpose" to get her attention. He insists that they really get along very well. He tells me Cynthia says, "Wade, if you leave me, I will kill you."

In 1989, Cynthia dyed her hair pink because she wanted to be punk. Cynthia is forty-seven years old. She is missing some teeth and, over dirty brown hair, wears a cap that says *Cancun Mexico*. She also wears a windbreaker, pink gloves, tennis shoes, and a white t-shirt. She has no government income.

Donna also known as "Puffy"

January 25, 2006, mid-afternoon
Wilshire Boulevard

Donna walks with Timothy, her husband, both pushing shopping carts with their belongings inside. Timothy is from Virginia and was a Marine. A strong smell of alcohol emanates from Donna. Donna wears a hospital bracelet. She suffers from hypertension and asthma and just got out of the hospital after an asthma attack. Donna's manner is accommodating and mild; she responds slowly to questions and comments.

She's been on the street for six years, four of them in Santa Monica. She came here and helped a man with AIDS. She went to prison for three years for committing an assault against this man; she was accused of trying to cut his throat. Donna is a two-striker.

She has no children. She says when she was thirteen, she was raped by five men. She is now fifty-one years old. I offer her two dollars, but she sees the end of a five-dollar bill peeking out of my pocket and asks, "How about that fiver?" So I trade her the two for the five.

Donna starts to cry when I ask if anyone from a social program has offered her assistance. She says no, although in the past she has been helped by two local organizations. She says she suffers from depression and anxiety.

On May 10, we see Donna and her husband sitting on a bus bench on Lincoln Boulevard. She looks a little different than before—very tired, less clean. She looks up the street without expression.

Marie
February 17, 2006, 11:40 a.m.
Wilshire Boulevard and Sixteenth Street

A man and woman, both white, are walking west on the south side of Wilshire Boulevard. They are arguing so loudly they can be heard on the other side of the street over the traffic. She stops walking; he goes on. He waits for her; she catches up. Her voice is thin and abrasive; she sounds angry. He pushes a shopping cart piled high with bags and also with bags tied around its sides. He wears a heavy backpack. She carries nothing. They cross to the north side of Wilshire.

I can hear her complaining and screaming at him that she can't go any farther—she has to eat. He offers to buy her food. She says she can't eat what he wants to get her. A bag of cheesy potato chips appears. She eats it. Crumbs cling to her mouth and chin and fall on her clothes. She is wearing baggy men's clothes although she is quite slight: a stained maroon long-sleeved shirt and pants. The shirt at first conceals that she has a cast on her left arm and also wears a hospital bracelet.

At Sixteenth Street and Wilshire they stop. She continues to say she is in great pain. I am ahead of them on the sidewalk and open the conversation, pointing out the emergency room across the street. All of a sudden her tone changes. She asks me if anyone has ever told me I look like Sharon Stone. I say no, that I know flattery when I hear it, and that I'm about twenty years older than Sharon Stone. I ask if I can talk to them and they say yes. The man in particular says he'd like to tell me about his life, that he has a lot to say.

He is soft-spoken and seems genuinely concerned about her. He offers her food and suggests ways to take care of her. I comment that he seems very considerate of her. He answers, "I'm a philanthropist." It is clear that his job is to take care of her and respond to her demands.

She says she just got out of Saint John's Hospital where she spent three days. She says she was raped and beaten up on Van Nuys Boulevard in the San Fernando Valley and that her arm was broken. She shows signs of being hit in the face. I ask her how she got to Santa Monica to be treated and she says, "I don't know." She points to the man and says he was so drunk he couldn't help her. He looks sheepish.

I ask how long they've been together and she says, "Two days."

Her name is Marie. His is Martin. She sits on the bus bench so we can talk. She has the presence of mind to put a piece of newspaper over the beer she is drinking and that she has set down next to her.

Marie grew up in Burbank. She attended Burbank High School but dropped out before graduating. She is forty-five years old and has a twenty-four-year-old daughter and a twelve-year-old son. It's been six years since she has seen her son. She says it's too hard to visit him—look at me, she says, how could I manage? She says I have no idea how hard it would be for her to see him.

Martin is eager to talk. He sustained a brain injury from a car accident in 1988. He seems a little slow, almost childlike. No matter what Marie says to him or in what kind of voice, he does not get angry; he tries to make her feel better.

Martin shows me a letter dated July 6, 1999, and addressed to him at a Winnetka, California, address. The letter is signed by the Director of Security at Rockefeller Financial Services, Inc., 30 Rockefeller Plaza, New York. The letter says:

"Mr. and Mrs. Rodman Rockefeller convey their appreciation for your thoughtful gift of art. However, it was decided to return your painting as requested, feeling confident that you will find a suitable location to display your work."

Martin insists that I keep the copy of the letter, saying he has many more. The copy is mildewed in the bottom-right-hand corner; otherwise, it is in good shape.

I will both lay me down in peace and sleep.

—PSALMS 4:8

Under a roof. In a bed. Where it's quiet and safe.
Knowing I'll wake up in the morning. Knowing there's help.
And hope. Having a plan for the future.

The Women of Daybreak

Sheba

February 28, 2006

Throughout our conversation, Sheba says in a low, sorrowful voice that she's "trying to get to that purpose, because I know there's a purpose for me in life."

Sheba says she is South African, that she was adopted by American parents when she was four and one-half years old, and was raised in Philadelphia. No one spoke her language when she arrived. She was wrenched from her culture. It got more difficult as she got older; memories triggered one another. Still, she describes herself as a happy child. She says she grew up in a "nice mixed group." Elementary school was good for her, although she didn't graduate from high school because she had learned what they could teach her. She wanted to find out about living on the street. She had to take that path. She is content on the street. She can survive there. She has been on her own since she was seventeen and one-half. She says she was outside "twenty-four/seven" in Philadelphia, Virginia, Baltimore.

Sheba was married to a Salvadoran and for six years they slept outside together. She has never worked a day in her life. A miracle, she says. She never paid taxes, never had a "nine to five." Now Sheba is looking ahead to what she can do. She hopes to work, be a receptionist, help people who are hurting. She says so far she has been "on the fast mule" and that means having a big load. She's trying to get to where she can unload.

The "load" she wants relieved is not knowing who her biological parents are and what traits she inherited from them. She wonders, "Could they have loved me? Could they have taught me more than I know? My purpose?" She hasn't seen her adoptive parents since she left their home.

Sheba has no children and doesn't want the responsibility of friends. She says she's really tired, physically and mentally. But she's not going to give up. At Daybreak, she makes art. Under one picture she wrote, "I'll be a part of this, and maybe being a part of this I'll find out something." And she did find something, she says: "I can be poetic."

Sheba has been in Santa Monica for ten years and at Daybreak for a year. She feels "content" in Santa Monica and has no plans to go anywhere else. She came as far as the water and plans to go no farther.

Gwen
July 20, 2006

Gwen speaks in a quiet voice. She is gentle in manner and seems delicate and vulnerable. She says she is by herself and comes to Daybreak for support; she likes the classes in jewelry making, art, and writing. She wants to attend one of the Daybreak discussion groups on housing to help her be able to talk to a landlord and manage her housing needs.

Gwen came to California from Brooklyn in 1986 because she had asthma and her doctor recommended a warmer climate. When she got to Los Angeles, she got a job and stayed with people she met. She gave her paycheck to these people, and they took advantage of her. When she got General Relief, they wanted that, too, so she left because she wanted to keep money for her own food. She slept at an aunt's home for a year or two, but couldn't find a job. In 1987, she left her aunt's and went to Las Vegas where she worked as a hotel maid at a Holiday Inn. When Gwen returned to Los Angeles, she stayed at a religious shelter. During this period she was assaulted and raped at a hotel. The police caught her assailant, but she was terribly frightened. This happened when she was in her twenties.

Gwen was born in Virginia, but raised in New York from the time she was six. She was raised by her mother with thirteen siblings. She was a middle child and had an identical twin who died of cancer when she was in her late thirties. Gwen says her mother was very strict with her when she was growing up and beat her with switches and belts. Her mother wanted to beat the meanness out of her. Gwen was always running from her. Her mother beat the others, too, but not as badly.

Gwen has had two semesters of college. She studied music composition, literature, and psychology, which she failed. She has taken psychiatric medications for years. She has experienced depression and fear and also schizophrenia. She says sometimes she feels closed in, like she can't get out.

Gwen has gone from shelter to shelter. She says she has had eight to ten shelter stays. She can't sleep when she's outside. In Los Angeles in the early 1990s, she got an SRO (single room occupancy hotel room) and stayed a year. She was only receiving General Relief, and she became very depressed and went to Denver in 1992 where she ended up in another shelter. She couldn't arrange for Supplemental Security Income because she kept changing addresses.

Daybreak accepted her and she can stay at the shelter for four to six months. After Daybreak she hopes to go to a transitional living program and have Section 8 housing. She says she had it once, but lost it two years later because her brother was staying with her. She says that as long as she keeps up with her mental hygiene and takes her medication and follows the rules, she should be all right.

Mary

Mary sounds like a stand-up comic when she talks. She delivers one-liners with the polish and timing of a professional. She knows she is funny.

Mary tells us she suffers from diabetic retinopathy. She can't see out of her left eye. She was treated by an ophthalmologist. She says this doctor blinded her, so she put a hex on him. The eight people who left his office before her also left blind. "You got some bad company, baby," she says. She wants to get a second opinion.

After she lost her sight in her left eye, she became very depressed and wrote a bunch of bad checks, about two thousand dollars worth: to markets and to some other places. Charges were pressed and she got a court date. She was so depressed she wanted to die and tried to get a bus to hit her, "but the damn bus wouldn't." She was treated at a mental health center—the "nut house."

Two years ago, while riding a ten-speed bicycle, she fell and broke her ankle. They "got me a new ambulance for this old body." She was on morphine for a month. She says people came to visit her to steal her drugs. Now she takes Tylenol each morning to kill pain. She says she still has twenty-nine screws and five clamps in her ankle.

Mary grew up in Kentucky and says her parents were college graduates. She says she doesn't know what the other women told me about why they were homeless, but the reason is the same for all of them: drugs. Plus whoring on Skid Row. She saw them and she knows what she's talking about.

Mary was on Skid Row in Los Angeles at Fifth and Crocker Streets. She smoked dope, pot, and rock. Cocaine had no effect on her and she didn't like it. She used to burn and inhale crystal meth. She says crystal meth is the worst—it's why people kill their parents. She doesn't use drugs any more. She says everybody was hanging out on Skid Row. When she was there, she was "packing. . .holding me a piece."

Mary is sixty-three years old. Thirty years ago she came to California from Cleveland where it was twenty-eight degrees below zero. She says she's not walking to the Section 8 office in knee-high snow. "I likes to be my evil self." Though as a child, she loved snow.

Mary says she married a fool, but "that's life." Her husband's name is Junior. She has been married to Junior for over twenty years. Before she married him, she says Junior was involved in a shootout. Later Junior murdered a blind Korean storeowner. Mary says he had "no reason to kill that man." He is now in prison serving a life sentence without possibility of parole for killing a five-year-old child in a dope house. Junior was a drug addict. They're still legally married because if she divorces him, she's afraid his gang will be after her. Junior has been in prison in West Virginia for the last twenty years. Mary says crime runs in Junior's family.

Mary describes herself as a "hillbilly." She's not into baked chicken—"I fry." She says she knows sign language and demonstrates with her left hand.

Before coming to the Daybreak shelter, Mary was outside for six months. She wears a rosary around her neck and black skull earrings. She wears a blue-and-green plaid muffler, clean jeans, and a green parka. Mary says all she has to do is "stay black and die."

Lourdes
March 9, 2006

Lourdes' mother was a Catholic who was devoted to Our Lady of Lourdes. Lourdes grew up in the Philippines and came to the United States in 1989 when she was forty-two years old. She went to New York first, thinking she would live there. The pictures of the Empire State Building and the snow had looked so nice, but it was too cold, and she never went out of the house. She came to California where the weather is better.

In the Philippines, Lourdes says she was a fully licensed pharmacist. She never married, although she wanted to adopt a child, but her father said, "No, take care of your own blood." She says she sees her family every five years when she visits the Philippines.

In California, Lourdes worked at a number of different jobs including caretaking for a blind and disabled man, who gave her a place to live. Lourdes says she had to stop working in September of 1997 because she was suffering from hypertension. At about this time, she started hearing voices that talked to her about acceptance and rejection, and she was diagnosed with schizophrenia. Now she takes various medications and tries to cope with the schizophrenia by ignoring the voices. When she stopped working, she was homeless for a couple of weeks and slept in a van owned by a cousin. She says her family can only help from a distance, with prayers. All her relatives are either busy or distant.

Lourdes learned through treatment that the schizophrenia comes from her father's side of the family. As a child she says she was stubborn. Sometimes her father used corporal punishment, but that was not abuse in the Philippines. It's the parental duty to correct children. She also says her father loved her, and when she was sick he took care of her.

After her diagnosis, Lourdes stayed in various hospitals and care programs for about a month. She has stayed in various shelters including Daybreak. She has lived in board-and-care homes and apartments, and she hopes to have a new living arrangement when she is a senior. Lourdes told of problems with each housing situation, including having her money stolen, having a hard time getting along with property owners and other residents, and experiencing a fire in her unit. Lourdes feels that people group together and plot against her, and she doesn't understand why.

One day Mormon missionaries stopped at her door. Because they were so nice and she liked what they said, she converted after her mother died, and Lourdes is a practicing Mormon now.

Lourdes keeps several bags with her, a couple of them quite heavy. One is a large suitcase on wheels that doesn't zip closed all the way. As she leaves us, she gets her bags together. She says she can manage. She'll pile one on top of the other and take the bus. She does it all the time. It's not a problem, she says. "I must struggle. I must be strong."

Pam
February 28, 2006

Pam is forty-eight years old. She has been in Santa Monica since 1979. She came here from Long Island to go to UCLA, where she was majoring in German. During her junior year abroad in Freiberg, Pam started hearing voices. Her sister flew to Germany to pick her up and bring her home.

Pam was diagnosed with schizophrenia. She said it was like having a radio on in her head. She couldn't tell what was real and what wasn't. She was in a hospital for five weeks and given medication; it felt like she was in jail when she was in the hospital. She said it was very scary. She returned to California and lived in her own apartment, although she was afraid people would think she was crazy and put her away. She still heard voices: they would read signs; on the bus, they told her to get off at the wrong stop. Reality wasn't reality—she hallucinated: sometimes when she looked at people, they turned into animals.

Pam is stabilized now. She takes medication that controls her symptoms. In 2005 she earned a B.A. in Spanish from USC. Through USC, she studied Spanish in Madrid during the 2004 spring semester. She still emails "La Señora," the woman she lived with for the semester. Pam earned her first two college A's at USC: in history and literature. It took her three extra years to graduate. In addition to English, German, and Spanish, she understands French and Italian. She would like to work in written or oral translation. She is currently taking classes at Santa Monica College.

Pam has had an apartment in Santa Monica since 1998. Before that, she lived in shelters for four or five years. Sometimes she didn't take her medication; in the shelter, they put her back on her meds. She stayed for a while with her brother, but he doesn't understand mental illness and is not empathetic. She now sees him once or twice a year. One of her sisters visits a couple of times a month.

Pam has learned to rely on herself and be independent. She is "into healing." She says she takes fish oil, flaxseed oil, olive oil, cod liver oil, and calcium. She believes in and practices preventive medicine. Because of the medication Pam takes for schizophrenia, she has gained a hundred pounds and it's been hard to lose. She's been fighting it for five years and the weight loss has been gradual. When she was living in shelters, it was even more difficult.

    She has lived in two local shelters besides Daybreak. Now she has a Section 8 apartment toward which she pays $160 a month of her Supplemental Security Income; HUD pays the rest. Pam still comes to Daybreak for fun. She says it's a very positive and nurturing place and she enjoys taking the art classes offered there. She'd like to learn to play the guitar. When she was in high school, she played basketball and volleyball, although she has played no sports since a car accident some years ago.

    Pam is calm and insightful. She thanks us for our interest.

Linda

Linda grew up in the Midwest and was married twice. She was a real estate broker and an appraiser with an M.A.I. designation, and in 1989 she had her own business. She qualified as an expert witness and testified in court cases. She is a college graduate. But she has suffered from depression her whole life. About five or six years ago, Linda had a major depressive episode and, as her depression worsened, she couldn't work. Her brother thought she was lazy and told her to get a job and stop feeling sorry for herself.

She stopped going out. She became isolated. She lived on her savings for a couple of years and lost her health insurance. Then she borrowed money. She was evicted for nonpayment of rent from her rent-controlled apartment north of Wilshire Boulevard.

For a number of years before coming to Daybreak, Linda sought help at two mental health centers, but she couldn't break out of her depression. She has tried different anti-depressants without success, but feels better now because she is no longer isolated. She has lived at Daybreak for six months. If she needs to, after she leaves Daybreak, she can go to a transitional shelter to help her adjust to more independent living. Linda is sixty-three years old and receives SSI and Medicare. Recently she was accepted to the Section 8 housing list. Priority for housing is being given to seniors, those with disabilities, and the mentally ill. She'll be able to take care of herself now. She feels safe for the first time in six or seven years.

Linda likes photography and has some photographic equipment in storage. She is white-haired, pink skinned, and has intelligent blue eyes. Linda is not her real name.

Sherry

February 28, 2006

Sherry is forty-four years old. She worked for a dialysis company in the billing and administration department as an administrative assistant, but had to retire due to mental illness when she was thirty-two. Work was too stressful. She is bi-polar and now stabilized and under medical care.

Sherry describes her parents as controlling and interfering with her desire to be independent, so at twenty-three she went out on her own. She wanted to get out sooner, but her parents wouldn't allow it.

Before her diagnosis, she was having troubles and trying to medicate with drugs. They didn't help. She had a breakdown, and her parents put her in a mental hospital. After her diagnosis, her parents took a class on mental illness; they wanted to know why she acted like she did.

She says it's okay to have mental illness, but that the hard part is getting the public to understand it. For example, her manicurist is afraid of her. He does her nails "really fast." He says, "You're not going to bring other ladies here with you, are you?" After he's finished, he won't let her sit long enough for her nails to dry.

Sherry has been taking medication for ten years. A couple of times she went off her medication, skipping a few weeks. She dabbled in drugs, but she is clean and sober now and has been for the last one and one-half years.

Sherry has had two and one-half years of college, studying photography and dance at Santa Monica College and Long Beach City College, but she doesn't have the patience for more school. She has lived in several shelters; she has been at Daybreak for nine months. Sherry's not sure what comes next.

Margaret

July 20, 2006

Margaret was born and raised in Santa Monica, and she went to Santa Monica High School until tenth grade. She is forty-eight years old.

Margaret suffers from post-traumatic stress disorder because of early abuse. She says she was sexually abused by a relative when she was eleven or twelve, raped a few times, and beaten up more than once. She experiences black-out rages where she wants to hurt herself. She has an anxiety disorder and brain damage because of her use of alcohol and drugs. When we speak, Margaret has been sober forty-five days. She had ten years of sobriety but lost it in 2003, and her minor children went to live with her mother, who is the legal guardian of the children. Margaret sees the children when her mother allows it. She has had four husbands.

She wants to be at Daybreak because of the mental health therapies available. She receives SSI. She takes medication for anxiety and depression. She was homeless in the late 1980s and early 1990s. She believes that the homeless problem can be solved by building more shelters. Margaret says there are a lot of mentally ill people and some programs for those who are "extreme in illness." There are others who can learn, do work, volunteer, be trained, etc.

Margaret says she knows people look down on "us"—meaning those who are mentally ill.

Lynda Lee
February 28, 2006

Lynda Lee is sixty-four years old and just broke up with her thirty-nine-year-old boyfriend—"a certified genius who went bad." Lynda Lee became ill in 1984. She was working eighty to one hundred hours per week as a legal secretary for a nonprofit organization. She worked there because she wanted to do something good, but she only slept three hours a night during the three years she worked there. During this time she remembered an assault she suffered in a hospital and began suffering from post-traumatic stress disorder.

In addition to her bad memories, Lynda Lee suffers from sleep problems, which she says her doctors would not recognize. She has had sleep tests that showed six different sleeping disorders. She also suffers from osteoarthritis and fibromyalgia. At one point she mentions "barfing her guts out" and not caring.

Lynda Lee was a good student in high school. Her verbal scores were off the chart. Now she is on disability, but she's "not going to lie down and die." She says she's not on parole or probation, not on crack, heroin, or speed. She gets tired. She tries to rely on self-help. She can't do chores. She says when she was sick, they wouldn't let her in the shelter, that they're not prepared for sick people. She is physically disabled. She says she's sick and fifty-seven years old and supposed to die, but she doesn't. She signed up for case management, but was too tired to see the director. She says her Section 8 housing expired and she was too sick to do anything about it. She has lived in the back part of a recreational vehicle, and for five years she lived in cars.

Lynda Lee is animated when she talks, speaking fast, moving from one subject to another, expressing strong opinions. Social service programs deliberately keep you homeless until you "jump through the hoop." To get assistance from the Department of Mental Health, you must take their drugs. If you don't, no services. She says that doctors may have stratospheric IQ's but they have no sense; they don't seem to know they're dealers for the pharmaceutical companies. She says medications mess up people.

The pace of her speech speeds up.

She really resents that she can't get housing and wants to start a charity. She'll call it "Angel Care" and it won't be affiliated with any other organization. It'll be an independent operation and she'll make money and get off disability, and get the government off her back. She'll rent an apartment for six or seven hundred dollars a month. Now she never goes anywhere. She's too tired.

Anna

March 9, 2006

Anna wants to get into *LA Extras* but first she needs $199 for photos. A couple of her friends got into it and they've been in television shows. Anna says she used to be a model in New York City; her stepmother had a clothing business, and she modeled clothes for her. She's no longer in touch with her stepmother and doesn't want to be.

Anna was born in Bellevue Hospital. She never met her biological mother and no one in the family ever talked about her. Anna is bipolar and suffers from post-traumatic stress disorder. She was given lithium but stopped taking it because it turned her into a "zombie." Now she takes a different medication and feels better; for example, "I don't cry when a guy rejects me." Anna was routinely physically abused by a violent father who went to prison for assaulting her stepmother. He told her she brought the abuse on herself because she did something bad.

Anna first had psychiatric care when she was five years old. The psychiatrist came to her school for five years.

After her father was in prison, Anna stayed with her stepmother. One year they lived in Colombia because the manufacturing facilities for her mother's clothing business were there. They lived "in a penthouse." Anna says the manager didn't like her because she used up a lot of towels. She had a generous allowance and she invited her friends over and treated them to food and swimming. She didn't go to school for a year when they lived there. They left because of the drug wars. When they returned they brought with them a "black market baby" whom Anna refers to as her sister.

When Anna was thirteen, her stepmother kicked her out of the house. Anna went to live with her biological father's family. She lived with an aunt for a year and didn't go to school, so Children's Services removed her from the home, calling it unfit, and placed her in a foster home. Later, she went to a second foster home and, at age seventeen, went AWOL with her boyfriend. Then he abandoned her. She had to quit community college and she had no money. She was walking down the street in the Bronx when she met a boy who invited her into his home. He became her boyfriend. His family took her in, and Anna mentions how nice it was that they took in somebody they didn't know.

Anna became a nanny to a baby in the family because the baby's mother was on heroin. One day the mother slapped the baby, whom Anna dearly loved, and Anna slapped the mother back, and the grandfather fired Anna. The grandfather said it was the mother's right to hit her child.

Anna and her boyfriend came to California and found telemarketing jobs, but they didn't stay together. She got better jobs and traveled for her work. It was 1981, she was twenty-one years old, and in six months she made sixty thousand dollars. She worked on commissions and had no vices except drinking. She had to take care of herself, and she did. She lived in beautiful places—among them, Morro Bay and South Lake Tahoe. In 1984, she was in a car accident and couldn't work for a while. She met a man who gave her drugs and, for a number of years thereafter, she made her living making and selling amphetamines.

Anna has four children: Michelle, now eighteen, who is on the street; Paula, age sixteen, who is a good girl and lives in Southern California; Brandon, who is twelve and is doing well. Her fourth child, Destiny Faith, is five. The court terminated Anna's parental rights for Destiny Faith, although Anna says she didn't agree to it. She has great regret that she has failed her youngest child. The father of Michelle and Paula has been in and out of jail; Destiny Faith's father is a lifer. Brandon's father is a good man: he takes care of both Brandon and Paula.

From 2000 to 2005, Anna was incarcerated. She got out on November 7, 2005. She recently got off parole. First she was in jail at the Twin Towers in downtown Los Angeles and from there she was transferred to Chowchilla Women's Prison, which houses four thousand women. She says she had no money and was afraid she wasn't going to make it in prison. She says you have to have money in prison to make it. People from outside put money in her jail accounts for her. She went to jail for financial fraud including credit card fraud although she "never stole from the poor, only the rich."

Although Anna has been in and out of rehabs, she is now clean and sober. She goes to meetings and follows the Twelve Steps.

Anna is trying to turn her life around. She lived in transitional living for six months in a local program and in a shelter for six months where she was president of the resident council. Being president means she must set the example. Problems come to her and she takes them to the resident director. Some liked her; some didn't. She says it didn't bother her. At the shelter, she made sure people got what they needed like toiletries and other supplies. She also tried to ease confrontations. When she needed direction or assistance, they gave it to her.

After she "graduated" from the shelter, she was asked to come back as a volunteer staff member. She is learning money management. She goes to meetings. She is a part of it; she follows the rules. She says she got barely any conduct reports. She was comfortable at the shelter. She felt safe. She wasn't afraid and didn't get involved with the wrong people. People at the shelter helped. She was very tired of being on the streets. It was exhausting.

Anna's future plans including housing. After Daybreak she will stay at a transitional shelter to help her adjust to more independent living.

Anna says she has a need for speed. By "speed" she means excitement. She says if she were younger, she'd join the military and try to fly jets. Or be a racecar driver. Or, if she can get a sponsor or a grant, she might open a shelter herself.

Elizabeth

July 20, 2006

Elizabeth likes to paint "relics": old things, collectibles of World War II vintage and before; also cactus flowers. She is fascinated by blooms. She uses only watercolors. Elizabeth says she dreams in color.

In 1945, Elizabeth started grammar school in Glassell Park near the Arroyo Freeway. There was an art staff at the school, and they taught children with exceptional talent, and Elizabeth took art lessons. She painted underwater scenes. After grammar school, she attended Benjamin Franklin High School.

She attended nursing school at BYU for two years and worked at Cedars of Lebanon in the cardiac care unit as a nurse's aid. She didn't like lifting trays. They were heavy and she's small. She had a nursing license from the state of Utah. Later she went to work in banks and at brokerage firms where she was a broker. For a time she was a mutual fund trader, and a member of the National Association of Securities Dealers. She worked in Burbank, among other places.

She developed ulcers and psychosomatic illnesses including insomnia and anorexia. She took sleeping pills and Valium for her ulcers; both medications were addictive. For about five years she took prescription sleeping pills and then began missing work.

When she was living in Burbank, she was burglarized. She also suffered a concussion and had to take drugs for seizures. This medication made her sleepy all the time. She worked part-time from 1972 to 1973 at bookkeeping and accounting.

In 1975, her father died of a heart attack and his life insurance went to his second wife; then her Uncle Steven died. Elizabeth says "so many things happened at once." She developed a paralysis to the right side of the heart, which restricted the jobs she could take. She became partially disabled. She became homeless, and suffered from depression. Elizabeth began receiving Supplemental Security Income. She says the Supplemental Security Income laws penalize those who work. She tried living with roommates, but that didn't work out. In 1980 she became fully disabled.

She lived in a local shelter, which was very noisy. For the past eight years she has had Section 8 housing. She has never married and she has no children.

... at evening you shall say, "Oh, that it were morning!" because of the fear which terrifies your heart, and because of the sight which your eyes see.

—DEUTERONOMY 28:67

Hiding in a corner or under a bush to sleep; claiming a bench or a deserted alley. Hearing what you don't want to hear. Feeling what you don't want to feel. Hoping to wake in the morning.

...do not forget the things your eyes have seen or let them slip from your heart...

— DEUTERONOMY 4:9

So many homeless women. Do not
let them disappear from memory.
Do not let them be forgotten.

FEBRUARY 10, 2006

1:45 p.m. Santa Monica Boulevard
Black woman on bus bench, bent over. Looks like she has no teeth. Middle-aged. Thin. Short hair in disarray. Smoking. Shopping cart by her side overflowing. Bags on bench next to her.

1:48 p.m. Lincoln Boulevard
Asian woman. In front of Osco's. Filthy. Carrying bags. Walks with her eyes down. Skin looks unnaturally darkened by sun exposure. Maybe in her forties. Not sure.

1:50 p.m. Lincoln Boulevard
Woman with man. He's pushing cart with stuff. She's pushing a bike, wearing a backpack. She's in her thirties. Chubby, blonde, wearing dark clothes. They look unkempt, dirty. Both white.

1:55 p.m. Lincoln Boulevard
Filthy skinny woman, wearing crazy hat and scarf, boots, short skirt. Standing in traffic lane. Bowing and gesturing to traffic. Starts to wander out further and seems to realize it's dangerous. Goes back. Seems completely disoriented. Maybe in her forties.

2:35 p.m. Lincoln Boulevard
Woman pushing a child's stroller packed with goods. She has a brown pony tail. She's white. Wearing a colorful t-shirt. Thin, could be in her forties. Looks like missing some teeth.

FEBRUARY 15, 2006

12:41 p.m. Wilshire Boulevard
White woman pushing cart.

12:45 p.m. Wilshire Boulevard
Black woman sitting on planter wall, looking down, in courtyard of building on south side of street.

12:46 p.m. Wilshire Boulevard
White woman, scraggly brown hair, sitting on north side of street on building ledge with three men.

12:47 p.m. Wilshire Boulevard
Black woman pulling shopping cart laden with things.

1:28 p.m. Lincoln Boulevard
A woman and a man wearing matching jackets in an autumn leaf pattern with bags, standing on corner. Appear to be in late thirties, white.

1:49 p.m. Lincoln Boulevard
Black woman on portable chair on sidewalk with bags. At Vons, looks to be in her fifties.

1:51 p.m. Lincoln Boulevard
Black couple. He was pushing cart.

2:00 p.m. Palisades Park
About forty-five, of whom four are women, waiting for a meal at the HOPE feeding program.

Mid-afternoon, south of the Pier
Woman sleeping on grass, bags nearby.

Mid-afternoon, on walkway near carousel
White woman with shoulder-length gray hair doing knee bends and making irregular and erratic motions. Possessions nearby.

Mid-afternoon, Colorado Boulevard near Ocean Avenue
Blonde young woman, apparently in her thirties, wearing a straw hat and eating fast food in a doorway.

FEBRUARY 17, 2006

10:00 a.m. Wilshire Boulevard near Yale Street
Heavy-set woman, looks like Pacific Islander, sitting on bus bench on north side of the street. Wearing khaki shorts and baseball cap. Clean and handsome. Probably in her thirties or forties; plastic bag next to her on bench. Beautiful skin. Well groomed, scarf around neck, white tennis shoes, drinking something out of bag.

10:47 a.m. Wilshire Boulevard at Eleventh Street
Black couple. He pushing stroller filled with stuff; she sitting on ledge. Looks like they are arguing. He walks away from her. He's lean; she's heavy. In late forties or fifties.

10:49 a.m. Fourth Street and Santa Monica Boulevard
Stout white woman, probably in her thirties, wearing shorts and carrying a heavy backpack.

10:50 a.m. Seventh Street and Broadway
Woman in her sixties, wearing two hats, carrying two purses, wearing big glasses, backpack.

10:58 a.m. At Main Street and Strand
Woman standing with workers by catering truck on west side of street. Filthy, wearing red scarf, missing teeth.

11:10 a.m. Olympic Boulevard and Eleventh Street
Heavy-set woman getting ready to cross street, pushes brimming shopping cart into street on south side. Appears to be an Indian from South or Central America; wearing white long-sleeved shirt, wide-brimmed straw hat, long black pony tail down her back.

FEBRUARY 21, 2006

2:23 p.m. Vons parking lot at Lincoln Boulevard and Broadway
Young woman, sunburned, jeans, brown hair, thirties or so; have seen her before walking down streets, usually in the gutter.

2:24 p.m. Vons parking lot at Lincoln Boulevard and Broadway
Latina at outside table; long black hair, shopping cart, bags, thirties or forties.

2:27 p.m. Fifth Street across from main post office
White woman walking with three men. Sitting on sidewalk and leaning against wall of parking lot. Has backpack; wearing hooded sweatshirt.

2:31 p.m. Fourth and Arizona
Woman on sidewalk, missing teeth, red-and-white pants, messy brown hair, forties.

2:50 p.m. Third Street Promenade
Black woman in jacket and baseball cap with salt-and-pepper hair picking at her hands as she walks along. Activity appears compulsive. Looks agitated and distracted. In her fifties. Shuffling along.

2:55 p.m. Third Street Promenade
Overweight, young woman, maybe in her thirties, probably combination of Asian and Hispanic. Smoking. Neatly dressed though in clothes that don't match. Wearing a pair of jeans that are far too tight. Sitting on bench with obviously homeless man. Has been visiting with other homeless on the Promenade, notably the panhandlers who are there frequently. Seems to know many of the homeless people around her.

3:00 p.m. Third Street Promenade
Woman sitting inside shopping cart being pushed by man down Promenade intersection at Santa Monica Boulevard. Both in their thirties. She is very fair-skinned and wearing a hooded orange sweatshirt. Her face is covered with inflamed pimples.

3:25 p.m. Fourth and Arizona Streets
Black woman sitting on bus bench, middle-aged, possibly elderly. Probably wearing wig. Wearing a black felt hat. Handsome, neatly dressed. Watches us as we walk by and keeps watching us as we go north on Fourth Street to the parking lot entrance. We look back as we go in; she is still watching us.

3:38 p.m. Wilshire Boulevard at Eighteenth Street
On the south side of Wilshire, a white man and woman, tall, slim, possibly in their forties, walking west together, each wearing heavy backpack, matching heavy jackets.

FEBRUARY 27, 2006

1:03 p.m. Wilshire Boulevard at Euclid
Woman stands under eave of Vons Market to avoid rain. Middle-aged, long hair—white or blond, couldn't tell. Wearing all black. Has luggage on wheels.

2:05 p.m. Wilshire Boulevard near Nineteenth Street
Asian woman crouching on sidewalk underneath eave of store on south side of Wilshire. Looks very young, probably in her twenties. Wearing black hat, like a tam. Shoulder-length black hair. Has shopping cart crammed and overflowing with goods.

2:08 p.m. Douglas Park at Wilshire and Twenty-fifth Street
Black woman wearing two headpieces (black and white) is standing under wooden structure near restroom. Watching rain. May have spoken to her before. Couldn't tell, but headgear looked familiar.

MARCH 1, 2006

2: 45 p.m. Palisades Park
White woman lying on the grass under a tree. Sleeping bags, other possessions with her.

3:00 p.m. Palisades Park
White woman in her forties or fifties. Head covered with knit cap. Beautiful huge clear blue eyes. Skin very tan from living outside; unlined. Carries a bag and a bedroll. Wears dark jogging pants, a dark jacket.

3:15 p.m. Third Street Promenade
White woman in her thirties, skinny, talking to herself. Blue eyes, walks haltingly like her right leg hurts, almost limping. Spitting as she walks. Won't talk to me. Has shoulder-length bleached hair, dark roots showing, bangs. Complexion broken out.

3:17 p.m. Third Street Promenade
Overweight woman in her forties with below shoulder, brownish hair. Carrying backpack. Stands in front of Barnes and Noble; goes in.

3:20 p.m. Third Street Promenade
Young; long, pretty, clean hair. Looks just washed. Some pulled back from either side and knotted or held with rubber band in back. Rest of hair hangs down. Has pretty curl at the bottom. Carrying a backpack. In her thirties.

4:00 p.m. Colorado Boulevard near Santa Monica Place
Beautiful black woman wearing well-applied and obvious makeup. In her twenties, head covered, bumps on her skin show through the makeup. Walking west toward the ocean. Looks ahead or down. Doesn't make eye contact. Carrying heavy pack.

MARCH 14, 2006

2:00 p.m. Palisades Park near brick walkway to overpass
Thin, very thin woman with platinum gray hair in a ponytail, wearing a warmup suit, silver hoop earrings, very tan face, beach walkers on a cool day, hurrying toward overpass and down to the beach.

Afternoon, Palisades Park
White woman, probably in her seventies, with a baby stroller full of belongings including a large red teddy bear.

MARCH 22, 2006

2:30 p.m. north side of Wilshire Boulevard at Fourteenth Street
Black woman, probably in her fifties, with hair below her shoulders pulling heavy suitcase on wheels.

3:00 p.m. Ocean Avenue in front of the Wilshire Palisades Building
Black woman, wearing a turban-type hat, ski parka, tight pants, pulling a large heavy suitcase on wheels and wearing a backpack, talking to herself. She sees me look at her and releases a string of profanity and hostile looks in my direction. Probably in her forties.

3:30 p.m. Third Street Promenade
Black woman, toothless, wearing ski hat, loose clothes, dances to street singer. Dances to "Over the Rainbow" and three other tunes. Keeps perfect time, gestures matching each beat. At the end of one song, she bends over and bows, resting her hands on a nearby metal sculpture. About forty.

3:40 p.m. Third Street Promenade
Skinny white woman in boots, heavy make-up, long, dyed hair pushed under hat, wearing tight blue-and-white leggings, carrying backpack.

APRIL 21, 2006

11:00 a.m. Third Street Promenade
Two women on the Promenade filling out job applications in front of two different retail stores, both in late thirties or early forties, white, clean, bags nearby.

1:00 p.m. Third Street Promenade
Two black women with a man sit on a metal bench. They are surrounded by bags. They are eating and laughing. The younger of the women, maybe in her thirties, chatters, laughs, stands up. She wears a pink ski hat. The older woman is heavyset and has shoulder-length hair in an elaborate hairdo. It may be a wig.

2:00 p.m. Third Street Promenade
A white woman in her fifties with regular, attractive features walks down the Promenade. She is thin, has brown shoulder-length hair. She is very tan, probably from living outside. She carries two large plastic tote bags, one brightly patterned. I ask if I can talk to her. She says, "No," in a high, squeaky voice, and keeps on walking.

APRIL 26, 2006

4:00 p.m. Palisades Park
Down the way from the group of people waiting to be fed near Wilshire Boulevard, three women: one in her thirties, long, dyed blond hair, stout, tall, carrying bags; one in her thirties or forties, scraggly brown hair, sitting on ground with two men; one sitting on grass by herself near sidewalk, young, pretty, with bags, and filthy feet in sandals, slightly deformed toenails.

APRIL 28, 2006

Noon. In front of OPCC at Broadway and Seventh Street
Six women are outside on the sidewalk. One leans against the building; one is asleep; one eats in front; one older black woman has a shopping cart; another black woman sits on a bench; one has a sleeping bag. The one who is eating asks us, "What are you doing?"

3:30 p.m. Palisades Park
A woman in a hooded sweatshirt sits alone by the cannon near the Pier.

MAY 5, 2006

10:45 a.m. In front of OPCC at Broadway and Seventh Street
A woman in her sixties knocks on the Daybreak door. She leans against the wall. She is skinny, unkempt. She rings the bell. A heavy-set black woman answers. They swear at each other, argue. The older woman goes in.

11:00 a.m. Olympic Boulevard at the south end of the bus yard
A woman sits on the sidewalk and leans against the brick wall which surrounds the bus yard. Her possessions are around her in bags. She wears an orange top and appears to be in her thirties.

MAY 10, 2006

2:20 p.m. Palisades Park
A middle-aged black woman sits on a bench near the Senior Recreation Center. She is wearing a pink sweatshirt with the hood over her head. She wears another head-covering underneath. It is cold and windy, and she is bundled up. I have seen her before. She has a cart full of bags. Congenially, she says she "can't talk because I have to do my bills."

3:14 p.m. Bus bench on Lincoln Boulevard
A drunk and happy white woman sits with two men, one black and one white. "We're going straight," she calls out to me.

3:40 p.m. Douglas Park
On the corner, a middle-aged woman wearing a dark jacket hunches over.

3:40 p.m. Douglas Park
A white woman with a shopping cart full to the top stands in the park. She is thin, but notably pear-shaped from the back. She has brown hair and wears a short-sleeved red shirt.

SEPTEMBER 21, 2006

10:30 a.m. Palisades Park
Two men and one woman. She is thin, agitated, white, with brown hair. She appears to be in her twenties. She folds up her blankets; she has some cardboard in the bushes.

OCTOBER 25, 2006

8:25 a.m. In front of OPCC at Broadway and Seventh Street
A parked gray van full of people. Mary, whom we've talked to at Daybreak, is one of the passengers, all of whom are black. Mary says they are going to a court-ordered drug rehab program. She says don't talk to the other women as they are "very rough." I try to talk to one who tells me she's "not interested." The others don't look up at me.

8:30 a.m. In front of OPCC at Broadway and Seventh Street
A black woman, very skinny, wearing a hat and coat, walks by herself, looking at no one.

Acknowledgments

Thank you to the many people who allowed us to interview them and who shared their time, knowledge, and experience. Certain individuals stand out here: Richard Bloom, Ed Edelman, John Maceri, Robert Moncrief, Robert Myers, Jean Sedillos, Paula Villegas, and Lou Ann White. We also offer special thanks to Amy Turk, who invited us into the warmth and dignity of Daybreak and gave us unmonitored access to its residents.

Ari Rosmarin provided excellent research assistance. Working in a small and stuffy room in temporary library headquarters, he reviewed, copied, and organized twenty years of newspaper articles about homelessness. Recognition is due to Jessica Weiner, senior research librarian at the University of Southern California's Gould School of Law, for her comprehensive bibliography of legal and medical articles on homelessness and related topics.

We express our deep gratitude to Virginia Tufte—master teacher, master writer, friend—whose insights and suggestions greatly improved our work.

Theresa Accomazzo and Stephanie Palermini provided objective notes that also added to the project.

Maureen Noble contributed at every stage: editing, reviewing, organizing, marketing. Kim Dower enthusiastically presented the book to a wider audience. And, finally, thanks to Paddy Calistro and Scott McAuley of Angel City Press for imagining the form our material should take and for their considerable help in getting it there; and to Amy Inouye of Future Studio, without whom the book would not exist in such a beautiful state.

Blanket of Stars: Homeless Women in Santa Monica
By Frances Noble
Photographs by Ian Noble
Copyright © 2010 by Frances Noble and Ian Noble

Design by Amy Inouye, futurestudio.com
10 9 8 7 6 5 4 3 2 1

ISBN-13 978-1-883318-94-9

LIBRARY OF CONGRESS CATALOGING-IN-PUBLICATION DATA

Noble, Frances Khirallah.
  Blanket of stars : homeless women in Santa Monica / by Frances Noble ; photographs by Ian Noble.
    p. cm.
  Summary: "For more than a year, the mother-and-son team of author Frances Noble and photographer Ian Noble walked and drove the streets and traversed the parks and beaches of Santa Monica to interview and photograph some of its thousands of homeless women. The stories these women tell are heart-wrenching and hopeful"—Provided by publisher.
  ISBN 978-1-883318-94-9 (hardcover : alk. paper)
  1. Homeless women—California—Santa Monica. I. Title
  HV4506.C2N63 2010
  362.5082'0979494—dc22
                    2010012303

ANGEL CITY PRESS
2118 Wilshire Blvd. #880
Santa Monica, California 90403
310.395.9982
www.angelcitypress.com